CITY CRITTERS

how to live with urban wildlife

CITY CRITTERS
how to live with urban wildlife

by David M. Bird
Cartoon Illustrated by Sandra Letendre

Eden Press
Montréal

CITY CRITTERS
how to live with urban wildlife
by David M. Bird
with cartoon illustrations by Sandra Letendre

ISBN: 0-920792-59-6

Credits:
Cover design: Luba Zagurak
Cover illustration: Sandra Letendre
Page design: Evelyne Hertel

Printed in Canada
Dépôt légal — deuxième trimestre 1986
Bibliothèque nationale du Quebec

Eden Press
4626 St. Catherine Street W.
Montreal, Quebec, Canada
H3Z 1S3

Canadian Cataloguing in Publication Data

Bird, David Michael
    City critters

Bibliography: p.
ISBN 0-920792-59-6

1. Urban fauna.   I. Letendre, Sandra, 1958-
II. Title.

QH541.5.C6B47 1986   591.52'68   C86-090072-X

Dedicated to the memory of
Nik Pikes,
whose untimely passing at the age of twenty-one
cut short what would doubtless have been a
brilliant career in the world of canvas and brush

Table of Contents

LET'S GO TO THE MOUNTAINS THIS WEEK-END TO SEE SOME WILDLIFE!!

A NOTE FROM THE AUTHOR

Have you ever been rudely awakened in the wee hours by the clatter of tin cans on your driveway? Did you stumble downstairs and into the night to come face to face with a masked bandido or a striped night prowler armed with a spray worse than Mace? Has your garden or bird feeder become a fast-food outlet for a growing army of furred and feathered creatures ready to take advantage of you in a moment of weakness?

Virtually every urban or suburban dweller with eyes and ears cannot help but notice these days the impressive variety of wildlife species that have adapted to backyard life within our cities. It has become unnecessary to travel hundreds of miles into the country to be entertained by the antics of playful squirrels, the cool, composed manner of a foraging raccoon, the colourful flashes of feeding birds, or the purposeful flitting of a bat in the twilight. It's all there, right in our own backyards. Sometimes just a few alterations to your outdoor living space will not only provide more feeding and breeding habitats for wildlife, but will also serve to enrich your life.

Understandably though, we can all have too much of a good thing. Not everyone welcomes pigeons on the balcony, bats in the attic, snakes in the basement or gophers in the garden. You need not reach for your guns or poison, however. There are less drastic and essentially harmless methods available for maintaining peace with most city critters.

Whether you are cooperating or battling with backyard wildlife, there is always room for humour. With this in mind, I conceived the ideas for the cartoons in this book and presented them to Sandra Letendre. Sandy not only shared my humour by rendering them in pen and ink, but she also added a number of her own clever ideas.

We are fully confident that this guide to urban wildlife will provide a few chuckles, evoke a number of memories, make for light, easy reading, and become a handy source of ideas for time-sharing your property with some of the slickest, wiliest critters ever to hop, slither, run or fly across the face of the earth.

David M. Bird, Ph.D.

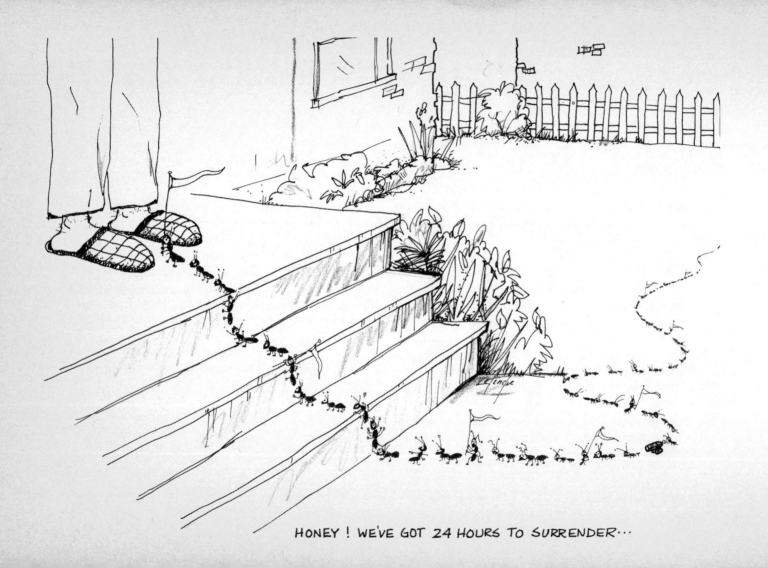

HONEY! WE'VE GOT 24 HOURS TO SURRENDER...

THERE'S WILDLIFE IN OUR SUBURBS

It was very gratifying for me to write this book, not in the sense of my duties as a wildlife biologist, but because I was essentially "weaned" on urban wildlife. During my pre-teen years in Downsview, Ontario, hardly a weekend passed that I wasn't chasing after some wild creature that lived in a ravine or park within the city limits. I often saw more wildlife during those afternoon sorties than you can see in days of hiking through our boreal forests.

The purpose of this book is to introduce you to some of the more common "city critters," the ones you're most likely to encounter in parks, ravines, and especially in your backyard. For most biologists, the term *wildlife* encompasses those animals with backbones (including fish) and those without, such as earthworms, crayfish, dragonflies, butterflies, and so on. I have opted to omit the fish and the invertebrates for two simple reasons. First, they are not often noticed in urban environments and second, I could not do them justice. I could have penned an entire book on urban and suburban insect problems. For that matter, hard-core wildlife enthusiasts will likely notice other omissions of animal species that are occasionally encountered in suburbia. Where streams, ponds and lakes exist in urban areas, it is not uncommon to see muskrats, bullfrogs, and painted turtles. Neither are cities off-limits to the odd deer, coyote, fox, or porcupine. Meadow voles or field mice are often found under old boards in vacant lots. As for the variety of birds found nesting in cities, we mustn't lose sight of the fact that since they have wings they can end up anywhere they darn well please.

I also hope to dispel certain myths about various wildlife species. This is evident, for example, in my lengthy treatments of the bat and the opossum, two creatures whose lore is steeped in myth and misconception.

Finally, I have approached the book with the philosophy that for every person who enjoys putting out suet for woodpeckers or providing seeds and nuts for pigeons and squirrels, there's another who loudly complains of the nuisance of urban wildlife. With this in mind, I have attempted to gather useful information not only for attracting wildlife to your neighbourhood or backyard, but also for preventing them from overstaying their welcome.

LOOKS LIKE ANOTHER BREEDING SEASON IS UPON US···

Urbanization is not new to North Americans. With the bulldozer supplanting the axe, it's just a heck of a lot faster these days. In spite of it all, various wildlife species continue to thrive amid a stark and sometimes unyielding concrete environment. Utility lines and sewer pipes become useful thoroughfares for these crafty critters, while streetlights attracting insect hordes subsequently bring in the toads, bats, and nighthawks. Urban green spaces like New York's Central Park and Montreal's Mount Royal become important stopover sites for migrating birds.

On the negative side, heavy and often ill-advised applications of fertilizers and pesticides on golf courses and backyards can poison urban wildlife. Exhaust fumes from vehicles and the use of salt or other de-icing compounds spell disaster for roadside vegetation and hence the loss of cover and food for wildlife. Many birds are killed each year in collisions with power lines, vehicles, walls, and windows. Uncontrolled pet dogs and cats can be a significant hazard to urban wildlife (and to people as well), often killing just for sport. When we complain of a little splash of bird feces on our cars, we would do well to remember that in New York City, dog excreta alone amounts to more than eighteen million kilograms per year.

Understandably, some wildlife species can become just a little too numerous or too cozy in and around our homes. In this book, I have deliberately excluded control methods such as poisoning or shooting, not only because most wildlife species are protected by laws at various governmental levels, but because I favour the use of preventive medicine. In other words, let's not give the critters a chance to become obnoxious in the first place. For example, tightly fitted lids on garbage cans or food storage containers make good sense to me. Pouring bleach, ammonia, Lysol, or even motor oil on your garbage will make it unpalatable for just about any freeloader. By trimming limbs near your roof and sealing all entry points into your home (including the chimney), you'll not only keep the wildlife in the great outdoors, you'll also save energy dollars. Appropriate fencing around gardens and netting over seed beds and small fruit trees can work effectively against your backyard becoming a restaurant for the furred and feathered. But why not grow a little extra for your "neighbours" anyway?

I can't emphasize the following point enough. *Not all the techniques suggested herein will work in every case.* They have indeed been successful for some people and are certainly worth a try, but it is not my intention to perpetuate myths. Cutting corners won't do you any good, either. For example, covering your chimney top with chicken wire won't prevent raccoons from nesting in there. They'll simply tear it off; a professional capping job is your best investment for the long haul. Before sealing up any entry points, it is always advisable, not to mention humane, to give any animals living in your home the opportunity to withdraw peacefully. The smell of a rotting carcass somewhere inside your walls, in your attic, or under your foundation may subsequently cause you to withdraw.

If your problem can't be resolved by any peaceful means, I strongly urge you to contact your local Humane Society, Society for the Prevention of Cruelty to Animals (SPCA), or a wildlife club or society. These organizations collaborate (or should) with specialists in wildlife rehabilitation, a field becoming increasingly popular these days. I recommend the same solution for those finding orphaned or injured wildlife. If your wildlife problem has become a serious threat to your health or your family's, I advise you to seek professional assistance from a pest-control operator.

Reflecting on a survey done in 1980 by Stephen Kellert, I do see an encouraging trend. Of the 181 Americans who suffered property damage from wildlife, only 28 percent resorted to poisoning, shooting or trapping to rid themselves of their problem guests. The rest used repellents and fences, or did nothing at all.

A national survey conducted in 1980 by the U.S. Fish and Wildlife Service revealed that eighty million people fed, photographed or observed wildlife around their homes. More than twenty-six million maintained bird feeders, each spending about twenty-two dollars a year on seed, while another fifteen million fed chipmunks and squirrels. Similarly, a survey by the Canadian Wildlife Service showed that just over twelve million Canadians fed, watched, photographed or studied wildlife around their homes in 1981. Of these, almost seven and a half million actually fed table scraps or store-bought preparations to backyard wildlife. In another survey by Kellert in 1979, almost 60 percent of the Americans inhabiting cities with populations exceeding one million felt that more tax dollars should be spent on programs to increase wildlife in urban areas. He also concluded that 25 percent of all American adults are bird-watchers.

In the above surveys it was apparent that songbirds, chipmunks, and squirrels were most enjoyed by urban residents. Anne Dagg, in her 1974 book *Canadian Wildlife and Man,* went a step further by interviewing 1,421 residents of the twin cities of Kitchener and Waterloo, Ontario. Fifteen percent of these people maintained birdfeeders, while 48 percent fed birds occasionally. Being diurnal, large, distinctively coloured, and relatively unafraid of man, the gray squirrel was the most frequently

WHEN ARE WE OPENING THE POOL, HON'?

seen city critter, and 68 percent of the people interviewed liked having them around. With the exception of gardeners, 64 percent enjoyed the presence of cottontails. The cutest, least obnoxious and therefore the most favoured city critter was the chipmunk. The skunk was the least appreciated. Few people noticed bats, but 18 percent of the homeowners liked having them around. Finally, birds were appreciated by 93 percent of those interviewed. The most commonly seen were the cardinal, goldfinch, bluejay, woodpecker, red-winged blackbird, hummingbird, oriole, flicker, and black-capped chickadee, in order of appreciation.

There is much urban residents can do to enhance wildlife populations in their communities simply by preserving or improving existing habitats, as well as creating new ones. Basically, wildlife has four needs: food, water, cover, and a place to live and reproduce. The first step is to keep around as much natural vegetation as possible. Mixes of deciduous and coniferous trees and shrubs of varying ages and with differing flowering and fruiting seasons are ideal. Instead of neatly manicured lawns, moist forest litter and plenty of undergrowth will provide much better cover for wildlife. If there's no danger from them, dead or decaying trees can be a source of food and nest sites for many animals. Minimizing erosion, preserving topsoil for re-seeding, and using compost or sewage sludge for fertilizing are essential for managing urban and suburban habitats for wildlife. A more productive alternative to sterile, concrete-lined ditches is to preserve existing streams with some buffer vegetation strips along the edges to provide travel lanes for animals. Recreational lakes and reservoirs are especially favourable for wildlife of all kinds. Finally, homeowners should be encouraged to plant flowers and shrubs, erect boxes and ledges for nesting, and undertake artificial feeding programs for wildlife, particularly in the cold winter months.

You might ask yourself why you should do all this. Well, I can give you several reasons. From psychological and sociological points of view, it is my firm belief that whatever wildlife forms choose to reside with you actually reflect your personality and even your social status (if this is important to you). Enjoying urban wildlife can consist of simply feeding pigeons in the park to taking a guided tour on a trail in a suburban park. Aesthetically, a neighbourhood and backyard comprised of the flashing colours of cardinals, bluejays, tanagers and goldfinches amid the greenery and flowers must surely be a more welcome sight to anyone's eyes than block after block of concrete and asphalt. Economically, it's a well-known fact that property values are increased by trees, shrubs, and flowers—especially if in close proximity to a permanent water basin designed to enhance wildlife populations.

AFTER 3 INNINGS OF PLAY — IT'S THE BLUEJAYS 4, AND THE ORIOLES 2 !!

Urban wildlife also serves as a useful barometer of a healthful human environment; obviously, one unfit for wildlife is also unfit for humans.

Most important of all, we must manage wildlife in urban areas not just for aesthetic, economic, and recreational reasons, but for its own sake. As you will see in the ensuing chapters, city critters are very interesting animals; they constitute an important part of our animal heritage.

THE SQUIRREL
is it a glorified rat?

Size:	Between 50 to 1350 grams, depending on the species, with the flying squirrel being the smallest and the gray the largest.
Colour:	Gray squirrels may be gray (salt and pepper, actually), blonde, white, black, and albino; red squirrels may be white-spotted, white, black, and albino; fox squirrels are reddish yellow with gray sides; flying squirrels are brownish gray; fox squirrels have rounded ears, the red is half the size of the gray; the flying squirrel has folds of skin that enable it to glide through the air.
Habitat:	Any treed areas, dens in tree hollows, woodpecker holes, leaf nests, attics, eaves, and birdhouses.
Food:	Nuts, berries, seeds, fruits, bark, insects, gourds, plant buds, peanut butter, molasses, maple sap, bones, meat, and salt.
Breeding:	One or two litters per year, with three to five young per litter depending on the species; fox and gray squirrels have two litters per year.
Active:	During the daytime, except for the nocturnal flying squirrel; they do not hibernate.

What ranges in size from a paltry 50 grams to a whopping 1,350 grams, comes in several colours, and is synonymous with *the* city critter? The squirrel, of course. On a stroll through many North American towns and cities, one might encounter, from smallest to largest and depending on its range, the diminutive but gutsy flying squirrel, the ill-tempered red squirrel, the early-rising gray squirrel, and the indolent fox squirrel.

The fox squirrel, recognizable from its rounded ears, is also shorter and thicker than the gray. The red is half the size of the gray, but makes up for it in sheer spunk. In all cases the sexes are similar in size and colour; the sex ratio is generally equal, but occasionally favours the males.

Fox squirrels have a reddish-yellow coat with gray on the back and sides. The red's name speaks for itself, but white-spotted, all white, albino, and black red squirrels are sometimes seen. Generally, the gray squirrel's salt-and-pepper appearance is the result of alternating bands of white, black and brown on each hair. The city of Baton Rouge, Louisiana, is home to a "blonde" race of gray squirrels, while the town of Olney, Illinois, attracts droves of tourists with its population of over one hundred white ones. For some unknown reason, albinos are especially prevalent in urban areas.

So where do all those black squirrels come from? Well, they're simply a variation on the gray squirrel, sometimes popping up unexpectedly in a litter from gray parents. Some regions, especially in northern latitudes, contain whole populations of black squirrels (like downtown Toronto). Unquestionably, the black fur allows less heat loss.

Noteworthy among many interesting adaptations is the yellow colour that develops in the eye lens of the gray squirrel. This yellow lens serves as a filter that improves vision and renders it high-contrast in bright light. A squirrel's 40° binocular vision and terrific lateral sight (the ability to see what is happening on either side) makes this a hard animal to sneak up on.

Thankfully, squirrels are devoid of musk glands, but they do have sweat glands between the pads of their feet; an excited or "hot" squirrel will leave wet tracks. A frightened squirrel can move at about 20 km/hr, with leaps of up to one-and-a-half meters. The grays are more agile in trees than the stumblebum fox squirrels. Occasional spills from as high as forty meters result in little or no injury. Leaping a span of two meters between branches presents no problem for most squirrels. The flying squirrel (which does not actually fly, but glides by using membranous folds of skin attached to its legs) has been known to glide from one tree to another one forty-five meters away, and to turn at 90° angles in mid-air. As for swimming, a gray squirrel can manage three kilometers in calm water, while the little red can even dive half-a-meter or so below the surface.

Those fluffy tails are what set squirrels apart from other urban rodents. Not only do tails serve as a balance (and occasionally as a parachute) for the squirrels' acrobatic branchwork and as a rudder during their infrequent swims, they also act as a sunshade in the summer, a warm bodywrap on chilly days, and as an extremely useful sensor for detecting air currents that indicate changes in weather or the entrances to holes. Best of all, tails can be flicked about in various ways to warn others of the extent of the squirrel's ill humour.

Fox squirrels are found in most midwestern cities and towns and are more likely to move into urban areas if no grays are present. However, one may occasionally observe the two species feeding in the same tree. The crotchety old male squirrels of all species keep to themselves, though.

The fox squirrel especially likes oak and hickory stands, and has been successfully introduced into numerous cities in the western states of Oregon, Washington, and California. If evergreens are present in an urban region, the red squirrel's range often overlaps with that of the fox squirrel, but ample evidence suggests that the former's aggressive nature seldom permits tolerance of either the fox or the gray squirrels in its territory. In short, when it comes down to food and den sites, the red is a tough competitor.

I don't have to tell you that there are a lot of squirrels out there. One woman living in West Lafayette, Indiana, live-trapped twenty-five on her lawn in one month. In 1971, eighteen were caught in another yard in just four days. Female fox and gray squirrels undergo estrus near the end of December and then again in June, producing two litters annually that average three young. Males will pursue an estrous female at a leisurely, lengthy pace over the ground and through the trees sometimes all day long, but with frequent pauses for rest and food. The female has the final say in whom she will mate with. The female red squirrel produces only one litter per year some time between March and May. Although she is receptive for only one day, she mates with several males without any preliminary courtship. She then chases them all off to raise her litter of four or five young by herself.

Weighing roughly fifteen grams at birth, young gray squirrels do not open their eyes until they are four to five weeks old. They become self-supporting after twelve weeks. In about eleven months, they're ready to produce a litter of their own. Now you know why there are squirrels all over the place.

Home-range sizes are quite variable, being dependent on the population density, the available food, and the sex of the animal. As a rule, males have larger ranges than females, and fox squirrels use more space than grays. Both the gray and the flying squirrel might use about half a hectare in most cases, but it could be as large as twenty hectares for the gray. The fox squirrel uses anywhere from four to sixteen hectares according to the season. The red squirrel falls in between its two larger cousins.

Sometimes a "fall reshuffle" occurs in gray populations between August and mid-December, where individuals might shift locations to places some sixteen to sixty-five kilometers away. By contrast, red squirrels are generally homebodies.

Squirrels live in loosely linked colonies. Seven or more individuals form a hierarchy, and the young make way for the old. At a concentrated food source, they maintain up to one-and-a-half meter's distance from each other.

WELCOME TA' DA' PARK. FOLKS !!

Unlike the lazy fox squirrels, grays are up and about before sunrise. However, they do spend much of the afternoon sleeping and sunning themselves. Except for the shy, nocturnal flying squirrel, the other species retire at dusk, but may come out on moonlit nights. Heavy rain or strong winds will keep a squirrel indoors. Depending on the weather, all four species are active year-round and do not hibernate.

It is impossible to describe their individual calls on paper, but generally speaking, reds are more vocal than gray or fox squirrels, and the barks of fox squirrels are softer than those of the grays. The juveniles of all species will scream loudly if removed from their nests. The seldom-seen flying squirrels are recognizable at night by their calls (high-pitched "tseets" at very short intervals over a ten-minute period) and by the pitter-patter of their feet on rooftops (the other species don't move along roofs as much and never at night).

In the summer, squirrels often take dustbaths to rid themselves of obnoxious insects such as fleas and ticks. Ironically, though, juvenile gray squirrels engage in an activity called "anting"; they will dig up an anthill and then roll and leap wildly about in it. Although squirrels keep their fur well groomed, the same cannot be said of their nests, which must either be frequently relined or vacated due to soiling. Both fox and gray squirrels use a combination of leafy nests (which are built in twelve hours but last up to three years) and more permanent tree cavities of eight centimeters in diameter. Grays are more dependent on the latter, and fox squirrels are content to construct their leaf nests in grapevine tangle or on top of Osage-orange trees (in the U.S.A.). Although highly dependent on woodpecker holes, flying squirrels in urban areas readily adopt attics, roof eaves and birdhouses as their homes.

In a nutshell, squirrels eat almost anything that comes in a nutshell, as well as berries, seeds, fruits, barks and insects. Of the hundred or so plant species eaten, the most staple are hickory, pecan, oak, walnut, elm, mulberry trees, and field corn. Fox squirrels especially enjoy the big fruits of the Osage-orange trees, as well as unripened gourds and tomatoes. Whole or partial ears of corn are carried to and eaten on an elevated perch or at the base of a tree (for the safety these locations afford). The acorns of black oak trees are less palatable to squirrels than those of the white oak. While gray and fox squirrels gnaw nutshells into fragments, the red is known to chew a dime-sized hole on either side of a walnut to extract the meat. The reds also commonly eat, among other fungi, the poisonous Amanita mushroom without ill effect, and they relish maple sap, obtained by stripping away the bark. As almost everyone with a bird feeder knows, they are not alien ground to any of the squirrels. One feeder attracted eight to ten flying squirrels every night.

Insects and their larvae are fair game. Besides sniffing out caterpillars from hickory bark, the clever gray squirrels have been observed in parking lots, checking out car radiators for dragonflies, butterflies, and grasshoppers, among others.

Here's a real shocker: squirrels occasionally eat meat. One gray squirrel was seen retrieving a stunned goldfinch (the bird had had a head-on collision with a window). A fox squirrel was seen catching and carrying off a sparrow-sized bird from a feeder. Red and flying squirrels are notorious for supplementing their diet with birds' eggs, nestlings, young cottontail rabbits, and even young gray squirrels. One bold red squirrel entered an owl's cache and devoured all the dead mice stored there. There's also the case of a flying squirrel that killed and ate a yellow-bellied sapsucker with which it was held captive—in the presence of food, no less.

Bones are eaten as well, presumably for the calcium they provide. Oddly, squirrels will also eat soil sometimes—as much as five percent of their diet, perhaps as a source of minerals. Licking salt off roadways and sidewalks that have been treated for snow removal is a favorite squirrel pastime, so a salt block in your backyard would be a real treat. Besides raiding trash bins for what, by a squirrel's standards, are tasty morsels, they also eat their own feces. With the exceptions of the flying squirrel and the red squirrel, who drinks frequently and even eats snow, water is consumed only occasionally, and is not really required.

The average gray squirrel eats about one kilogram of food per week, so they can be fairly hard on a bird feeder. Squirrels are renowned for hiding food. Caches have no particular ownership and communal hoarding is common. Sometimes stashed in tree cavities, nuts are most often well hidden four or five centimeters below ground and up to thirty meters away from the tree where they originated. Red squirrel caches at the base of trees, referred to as "middens," may be a half meter high and two meters in diameter. Although some memory is used to locate hidden stores, squirrels are capable of smelling them out, even under thirty centimeters of snow.

The annual mortality rates of gray and red squirrels are about 50 and 65 percent, respectively. It takes about seven years to replace an entire population of grays. Only exceptional animals make it to over six years old; one wild pregnant female was captured at twelve years of age. The tiny flying squirrel is lucky to hit its fifth birthday in the wild. Captive individuals of any species have lived to

BETTER CALL THE EXTERMINATORS, DEAR !! WE'VE GOT HUMANS !!

anywhere between eight and twenty years. Various preda-tors, winged and otherwise, include squirrels on their menu, but are unlikely to make much of a dent in their numbers. The major cause of decline in squirrel popula-tions seems to be a combination of mange mites, severe winter weather, and inadequate food supplies. Mange is a common affliction among fox squirrels (one animal was totally denuded of fur except for its tail and feet). A female gray, weakened from carrying over two hundred blood-sucking ticks, died instantly upon being chased. Fleas abound in squirrel dens, and in the fall, squirrels play host to abundant numbers of chiggers (mites that burrow under the skin). Some diseases transmissable to humans are carried by squirrels, but they are rarely transmitted. California encephalitis and tularemia (see the chapter on rabbits) have been reported in both gray and fox squir-rels. In the eighteenth and nineteenth centuries, pioneers described migrations of "billions" of gray squirrels that devastated crops and drowned in great numbers while attempting to cross large lakes and rivers. During a minor migration in 1968, extensive numbers were found dead on highways in the eastern U.S. A good number of squir-rels become road fatalities; gray squirrels seem to be particularly stupid around cars, waiting until the last moment to dash out under the wheels. Flying squirrels are so delicate that even rough handling can kill them.

OK, squirrels are interesting citizens, but one can't overlook the fact that they can also be a real nuisance at times. Many Britons will acknowledge that the gray squir-rel, which was introduced there in the thirties, is second only to the Norway rat in destructiveness.

For example, squirrels can be the bane of gardeners, destroying flower gardens, trees and shrubs. Besides peeling back bark to get at sap and insects, red squirrels also damage trees by nipping the buds from branch tips. Poking their noses into garbage bins is nothing compared to what squirrels will do if they get into a building; they will chew on all kinds of objects. Try sleeping at night with up to eight flying squirrels stomping around in your attic and gnawing the insulation to obtain nesting materials. Squirrels are fond of eating the insulation from outdoor electrical wiring and lead-covered telephone cables. While travelling the powerlines, more than one squirrel has shorted out a transformer, much to the delight of the neighbourhood.

As stated above, squirrels love bird feeders, rising to almost any challenge a bird lover may put in their path. One person hung his feeder by a single strand of wire greased with lard, but to no avail. After several determined squir-rels slid down the wire, hit the feeder, but bounced off, one finally managed to hang on to clean the feeder out.

DOES HE GET INTEREST ON HIS CACHE??

If squirrels are sharing your home with you against your wishes, you have only to seal up the entry hole (likely under an eave or down your chimney) with 1.2 cm wire mesh while they're out during the day. If there are young in the nest, it would be humane to wait until they have vacated the premises. The liberal use of moth balls (napthalene) or moth crystals (paradichlorobenzene) in tight spaces (see the chapter on skunks), access by the family cat, or a continually burning light may keep squirrels out of the attic. Of course, preventing entry by trimming branches close to the roof will nip a potential problem in the bud. Speaking of which, encircling tree trunks or birdfeeder poles with a sixty-centimeter wide sheet metal collar placed 1.8 meters above the ground will thwart even the most agile squirrel. You can also string a series of pie plates or smooth sheet metal discs with a hole punched in the centre along the wires supporting the birdfeeder. Wire travel can be curtailed by installing sixty-centimeter sections of split plastic pipe five or six centimeters in diameter over the wire because the squirrels will avoid these sections of unsure footing.

To distract squirrels from chewing insulation or entering your birdfeeders, the idea of supplementation, that is a salt block or a less expensive food supply on the ground below, often works. Apparently safflower seeds are enjoyed by some birds such as cardinals, but not by squirrels.

If you've really got a problem with squirrels, peanut butter and molasses as bait works like a charm for live-trapping them. They should be released at least ten kilometers away, though, and preferably on the other side of a raging river.

I'm going to assume for a minute that there are some people out there who don't think they have enough squirrels in their neighbourhood. If you want to attract them, planting Osage-orange hedges, shrubs and vines along fencerows will draw in fox squirrels (but only in places where you might expect to find them), while extensive growths of conifers will attract red squirrels. Over-mature and large-crowned trees, particularly the varieties named earlier on, along with clear ground underneath them, will be most attractive to squirrels. The erection of birdhouses in oak and hickory stands within urban areas will bring in flying squirrels. Red squirrels will homestead in boxes 15 by 15 by 30 centimeters deep with a 4.5 centimeter hole. Finally, maintaining a birdfeeding station or growing a little corn doesn't hurt either.

As to whether squirrels are nothing more than glorified rats, I leave that up to the reader, but I've often wondered how they would fare in our eyes were they born without those wonderful tails.

THE CHIPMUNK
a charming panhandler

Weight:	70 to 115 grams, usually about 95 grams.
Colour:	Reddish brown with five black stripes and a white or buff belly, they can also be albino, black, or even white-spotted.
Range:	East of the Great Plains from the Gulf of Mexico to the southern tip of James Bay.
Habitat:	Underground dens with tunnel systems, hardwood forests, especially beech and maple, outbuildings, brush piles, rocky foundations, basements.
Food:	Elm buds, berries, hard nuts, foliage, bark, certain mushrooms, larvae, worms, snails, slugs, butterflies, dragonflies, eggs, reptiles, fruit, meat, plant bulbs.
Breeding:	Two litters per year of three to five young.
Life Span:	About two years.
Active:	During the day; not a true hibernator.

It is indeed a great pleasure to write about a creature that has invaded the human domain without making a major nuisance of itself. The chipmunk is such an animal. Few easterners with any interest in nature whatsoever have not experienced the greedy, but delightful antics of this tiny panhandler as it scurries back and forth with booty begged from willing victims.

The chipmunk's range extends over North America east of the Great Plains from the states bordering the Gulf of Mexico north to the southern tip of James Bay. You're likely to find this species anywhere there are extensive stands of deciduous hardwood forests, especially mature beech and maple. Chipmunks also thrive near human habitations, readily taking refuge in outbuildings, brush piles, rocky foundations, and basements.

The chipmunk's distinctive coat is reddish brown, with five blackish stripes extending from the shoulders to the rump, and a whitish band between the two stripes on each side. The belly and the sides are buff to white. Occasionally, albino, black, or even white-spotted specimens are seen. Generally though, the size and colour of the sexes are similar. Their weight ranges from 70 to 115 grams, with a mean of about 95 grams.

Most intriguing is the chipmunk's ability to stuff enormous quantities of food inside its mouth pouches. Consider these records from four different chipmunks: 31 kernels of corn, 13 prune pits, 70 sunflower seeds, and 32 beechnuts. Naturally, all sharp edges are bitten off the nuts before cramming them in.

Many people have been scolded by this chirpy creature's high-pitched chatter, complete with tail jerks to punctuate the remarks. Apparently, the chipmunk can issue about a hundred calls per minute for up to half an hour. If the chipmunk is in danger, you'll hear a loud "chip" followed by a trill just before it scampers to safety.

As with most panhandlers, chipmunks are solitary and, in fact, are quite agonistic towards one another. Their social hierarchy is based on size, although females in estrus or with young can be very aggressive. One female in the latter category defended against both sexes a territory about forty meters out from her den entrance. Beyond that, there is some overlap in their home ranges. In some regions, adult males defend a home range of about .15 hectares. In ideal situations, though, you'll be lucky to find four or five individuals per hectare, with perhaps an increase of two animals during late summer when the young have entered the population. Since a given animal may spend its entire life in that small area, there seems little need for a strong homing ability. Chipmunks have been known to find their way home after being moved about half a kilometer away.

During the course of the day, the chipmunk will often pause warily as it goes about its business. Should something frighten it, a chipmunk can streak away at 3.3 meters per second. The tail is usually held horizontally, but an agitated or frightened chipmunk will stick it straight up into the air. The tail is also elevated during the animal's infrequent swims. Chipmunks can climb quite well, too. They cannot, however, leap from tree to tree as squirrels can, thus the ground is a preferred location for feeding.

Not a nocturnal creature, the chipmunk's day begins at sunrise and ends at sundown, with peak activity times in the early morning and late afternoon. For some as yet unknown reason, chipmunks are seen and heard less often in the summer, especially the late summer, than in the spring and fall. Perhaps their foraging and reproductive activities before and after winter are the reason for this.

Their dens are located underground, comprising extensive burrows, sometimes more than four meters in length and having one or two entrances. The entrances are usually

"DON'T HE JUST MAKE YOU SICK??"

well-hidden under a rotten log, old tree stump, rock, stone wall, shrub, or between roots. No pile of dirt will betray their presence because the chipmunk digs them from underneath, shoving or carrying in its pouches the loose soil from a "work hole," and then later plugging up the work hole. New tunnels are added every year, while some old ones are closed up. The tunnels are generally five centimeters in diameter and may extend for a meter below the surface. The nest chamber itself might be about thirty centimeters wide, with its bottom filled with stored nuts and seeds, sometimes up to six liters worth, covered over with dried leaves and grass. There are exceptions to this "ground" rule, though; one female chose to raise her young in a hollow three meters up in an oak tree.

Chipmunks retire to their burrows sometimes between late October and early November. They are not true hibernators as they live off stored food and not accumulated fat stores. The degree of torpidity (lowered body temperature and reduced activity) also varies among populations. Some animals become torpid for up to eight days at a time, while others are either semi-torpid or not at all. Apparently when a chipmunk awakens for either a snack or toilet duties (they're very clean about this), it stumbles around with its eyes closed just like some people do. During mild periods, some chipmunks will actually come out to forage in the snow.

Chipmunks emerge from their burrows to breed in late February or early March, though they will head right back in if the weather is inclement. The females undergo two estrus periods, one from mid-March to early April and the other from mid-June to mid-July. Most have two litters, each comprised of one to eight young, but most contain between three and five.

After a month the naked young, weighing all of three grams each, are born with their eyes closed. By the fourth week of life, the young are running around in the burrow just like the adults, but their eyes are still closed. Shortly after this their eyes will open and a few days later they leave the burrow. When the young from the first litter attain adult size (at about eight weeks of age), their mother chases them off to prepare for the next litter. Females will sometimes breed at only three months of age, while the males usually breed only a year later.

The average lifespan of chipmunks in the wild is about two years, but a number of lucky ones make it to three. Captive animals often live to between five and eight years; one female made it to twelve. Just over half of the adults survive each winter; less than half of the young do so.

Some chipmunks become road fatalities and, oddly, they've been known to hopelessly entangle themselves in certain vines like ground ivy. Although chipmunks have been seen feeding with red and fox squirrels, at least one was seen being killed by the former species. A few early-rising or late-retiring individuals end up as owl food, and certainly a number fall prey to hawks. Others may become the victims of snakes, raccoons, house cats, and perhaps even of Norway rats.

On the other side of the coin, what's on the menu for the chipmunk? Well, quite a wide variety of foods. In spring they particularly like the opening buds of American elms. In summer, berries and cherries are eagerly sought, while in autumn the hard nuts of the hickory, walnut, oak, beech, and hazel are prized. Chipmunks also eat green foliage and bark and are very fond of certain mushrooms. They're not just herbivores though, as their diet also includes insects and their larvae, worms, snails and slugs, butterflies, and dragonflies. Even moles, young mice, sparrows, juncos, swallows, starlings, birds' eggs, frogs, and salamanders are taken on occasion. Chipmunks have been seen chasing down and killing garter and red-bellied snakes that are half a meter in length. To wash down their food, chipmunks drinks a fair amount of water, which is sucked up, not lapped in the manner of dogs and cats.

Some of the items on the chipmunk's menu are things that a city-dweller would be glad to be rid of, but the chipmunk also likes the seeds and flesh of watermelons, apples, pears, peaches, grapes, canteloupes, and squash. They've also been known to eat the bulbs and corms of ornamental plants like crocuses, tulips, and lilies. As a gardener you might have cause to dislike this striped opportunist. There might also be cause for complaint if a chipmunk has taken up residence under your house or patio. The only effective, humane way to get rid of chipmunks is to live-trap them and release them elsewhere.

On the other hand, chipmunks are tiny and their appetites are not voracious enough to warrant their removal. Besides the usual mites, fleas, botfly larvae and roundworms, they're actually very clean animals. Overall, there have been few grievances about their presence.

Besides being easily observed in daylight, chipmunks can be quite tame, taking food readily from the hand, though they will bolt at the slightest provocation. With such a high aesthetic value, why not just give in to their panhandling activities and enjoy their company.

RACCOONS
love 'em and leave 'em alone

Size:	4.5 to 13.5 kilograms, with northern animals being larger than the southern ones.
Colour:	Brownish gray, with a ringed tail and a black mask; there are some variations such as reddish brown, black, white, gold, and albino.
Range:	Most of North America.
Habitat:	Dens six to twelve meters up in trees, houses, barns, garages, churches, drain pipes.
Food:	Just about anything, except raw onions.
Breeding:	One litter per year consisting of three to seven cubs.
Life Span:	About five years.
Active:	Raccoons are nocturnal and are not true hibernators.

Almost no other four-legged animal better epitomizes the nocturnal city critter than the raccoon. Just about everybody recognizes that brownish-grey butterball body, ringed tail, and the Lone Ranger mask concealing a pair of beady black eyes. A few color variations exist though, including reddish, black, white, gold, and true albino complete with pink eyes. Raccoons shed their fur in April for a lighter summer coat, but by late August new under-fur and guard hairs begin to grow in anticipation of winter.

Northern specimens are much larger than southern ones, though the average coon weighs in between 4.5 and 13.5 kilograms. One monster tipped the scales at 28 kilograms, stretching 139 centimeters from his nose to the tip of his tail. They are amazingly strong for their size; one raccoon with a good toehold in its den supported a 90-kilogram man by its tail!

Raccoons are undoubtedly built for close-in work on the night shift. Although colour-blind, their eyes are packed with light-sensitive rod cells that are responsible for the red, sometimes green, gleam captured in the glare of

headlights or a flashlight beam. Even though raccoons have exceptionally keen senses of hearing and smell, these take a back seat to their tactile abilities. Each foot is comprised of a naked sole and has five long, slender digits. There are four times as many sensory receptors in the forepaw as in the hindpaw.

Above all else, raccoons are well endowed with the smarts. Where food is concerned, they are very quick to learn how to open fasteners of all kinds, and will remember the techniques for up to a year without practice.

"Cute," "cuddly," "curious," "comical," and "lovable" are just a few of the words used to describe the raccoon. Let me add a few more: "mischievous," "tough," "cantankerous," "bold," "tenacious," and "vicious." In other words, a split personality. Should you approach one and it finds you uninteresting, the raccoon will simply waddle off. If you're foolish enough to corner one, though, you will be confronted by a hellish little streetfighter who is anxious to survive at any cost.

Show me a town or city without a tree-lined stream, old houses, garbage cans or sewers, and I'll show you a town or city devoid of raccoons. They prefer to make their dens between six and twelve meters up in leafy hardwood trees or softwood ones prone to dying and hollowing, but they are definitely not shy about homesteading in abandoned or even inhabited houses, barns, garages, small sheds, greenhouses, and churches. Sewer systems and drain pipes are also used, but large fields are avoided. Don't be fooled into thinking that the lack of a sizeable entry hole will foil them either, as raccoons are quite capable of enlarging existing openings or gnawing and scraping out new ones.

Raccoons are crafty and nocturnal. So, how do you know if you've got them on your property? First, look for scratches on the trees around your home. You might even find a few silver-tipped hairs clinging to the bark. Their beaten paths along buildings, walls and hedges are often strewn with aluminum foil, tin cans, bread bags, cellophane wrappers, and other garbage. In addition to tell-tale tracks in mud or sand, the best sign is a "scat station" or toilet on a log, stump or rock.

The densest population of raccoons ever reported was one per 0.10 hectares, or more than six hundred per square kilometer in Missouri. An Ohio suburb boasted 107 coons per square kilometer, while a Cleveland metropolitan park was home to one raccoon per two and a half hectares. A detailed population study of a Cincinnati suburb revealed about one animal per hectare, a number equivalent to a quarter of the human population there. Depending on the time of year, that is whether young are entering the community, you can expect a population density of approximately one raccoon per four to six hectares in an average city or town with adequate habitat and available food. The actual home range of a given raccoon depends on food resources, its age and sex, and even on the weather conditions, but radio-tracked city raccoons stayed within a range of about five hectares, usually five-and-a-half times as long as it is wide, due to the way towns are split up into streets and blocks.

It's only a matter of time before these clever creatures catch onto taking buses and taxis. Walking or trotting, with the rump elevated and the tail up at a sixty-degree angle, they're never in a hurry though, and hence miss nothing. Raccoons can motor along at about 25 kilometers per hour. They cannot maintain this speed however, so if one is stealing a shiny silver dollar from your house, you could indeed run it down. Some radio-tracked raccoons averaged between .6 and 1.2 kilometers per night, and one relocated yearling male travelled 265 kilometers in 164 days. Raccoons are excellent swimmers; they have been known to cross rivers and lakes up to three hundred meters wide. As expert climbers, experiencing difficulty only with smooth-barked beech trees, they can descend head or tail first and can jump from a height of twelve meters to land on their feet without injury.

The raccoon's day seldom begins earlier than one hour before sunset and lingers on until several hours after sunrise. For the remaining twelve hours, sleep is the order of the day. During sub-freezing temperatures and/or permanent snow cover, raccoons in northern regions generally enter a period of winter dormancy (not hibernation) from late November to early April. Occasionally a few days of temperatures above freezing will entice them out from their homes to seek food. Raccoons in warmer states and provinces are usually active all winter long.

Except during the mating season, raccoons are solitary, especially adult males. During temporary feeding aggregations, close contact is avoided. Young raccoons will sometimes sleep in tree crotches in twos or threes, and one winter den contained no less than 23 individuals. Under these circumstances, knowing whether your roommate is submissive or agitated is quite handy. A submissive coon will press its head, body and tail to the ground while retreating or, if wishing to stay, will expose its nape and rump while avoiding all eye contact. If you've angered a raccoon, look for a lashing or raised tail, bared teeth, flattened ears, raised shoulder hackles and arched back (these last will exaggerate its size). And if it's lying on its back while attempting to claw and bite you, retreat immediately!

I DON'T CARE WHERE YOU MET HIM··· HE'S <u>NOT</u> STAYING FOR DINNER!!

Best take heed though, of the low warning grunt or snort if you want to avoid the above situation. Knowing the several calls issued by a raccoon can be a help. In hand-to-hand combat, your ears will be assailed by all manner of growls, snarls, and hisses. Most often, contented coons with or without young make a "churring" or purring sound, but mating animals let loose assorted squalls and shrieks. A shrill, whistle-like scream indicates extreme terror or entrapment. In the fall, raccoons will call one another with shivering tremolos not unlike those of the screech owl. Whimpering and chattering sounds are characteristic of very young animals.

In most populations, the sex ratio is roughly equal, but some studies revealed twice as many males as females, possibly because the males move around a lot more. Although males are larger than females, determining sex is difficult at best. If you insist on knowing the sex of the animals on your property, look for a penis bone on the males and three pairs of teats on the females.

Males generally do not breed as yearlings, but as many as 60 percent of first-year females will produce litters. Some aspects of raccoon breeding behavior might seem sadly familiar. You see, raccoons do not really have mates in the normal sense. The promiscuous males are polygamous and will breed with as many females as will have them. The females, on the other hand, are very choosy—but to no avail. The male will stay with her for just a few days. She will not only remain true to him, but will raise the family on her own. Copulations may last from twenty minutes to a whole hour, but the female, generally passive during the event, may terminate the session by turning her head and baring her teeth.

The breeding season lasts from late January to mid-March. The gestation period lasts about sixty-three days. Most litters, ranging from three to seven cubs, are born in May. As said earlier, the female does all the caring for the young and will move them to another site if they are disturbed. Sometimes the entire family dens together for the winter.

Everyone knows that raccoons wash their food before eating it, right? Wrong. Only captive animals exhibit this behavior, and it has nothing whatsoever to do with cleaning or moistening food. This behavior is simply a substitute for "dabbling" or searching for aquatic prey in the wild.

It's a lot easier to list what raccoons don't eat than what they do eat because they will eat just about anything. Raccoons in an Ohio suburb consumed the fleshy fruits and seeds of forty-six different plant species, including some from gardens, garbage cans, and bird-feeders. They especially love berries, cherries and acorns. Crazy about

sweet young corn, raccoons barely finish one cob before starting another, breaking many stalks in the process. Virtually all reptiles, amphibians and small mammals (even rats, rabbits, squirrels, and kittens) can fall prey to raccoons. Crayfish, fish, beetles, and other bugs are also on the menu, and worms flooded from their burrows by rain are gobbled up like spaghetti. Unwary birds and their eggs are not immune either. Preying upon species as large as the great blue heron, raccoons will enter duck traps, kill all the occupants and feed on only one or two.

Raccoons can open ice chests and tightly fitted lids, as well as unlatch doors. One thirsty devil even managed to uncork a whiskey bottle pilfered from a camper truck. As for your garbage, they love leftovers. They will ignore raw onions, but you can use them as seasoning in cooked foods for them.

Wild raccoons seldom live longer than five years, but one wily critter reached sixteen. A Missouri population was totally replaced within seven-and-a-half years. The average lifespan of captive raccoons is ten to fourteen years, but old Jerry of Wisconsin died at the very ripe age of twenty-two.

Hunting, trapping and forest fires are prime sources of mortality. However, many juveniles succumb to malnutrition in late winter and to cars in the early fall when they leave their home ranges. The smallest predator of raccoons is the lightning-fast weasel, but larger ones include the great horned owl and the alligator.

Probably the best way to augment raccoon numbers in your neighborhood is to ensure the availability of den trees and plenty of wild fruit. Artificial nest structures such as nail kegs fastened in trees are readily accepted. If you want them real close, they are attracted to shiny or tinkly objects hanging on a string or, naturally, food with a strong smell. One couple nightly drew in a gang of twenty-two raccoons to a feast of cracked corn and dog biscuits three meters from their living room window.

If you want them at a distance, place hardware mesh over your chimney top, trim tree limbs that would afford them access to your roof, install electric fences around gardens and poultry yards, securely fasten garbage can lids, keep the cans in a raccoon-proof shed, and hang ammonia-soaked rags in potential den areas. The presence of a Doberman near your garbage isn't a bad deterrent either, as long as it doesn't jump in the pool with the raccoon; only the raccoon will emerge alive. Problem animals could be shot or poisoned, but live-trapping (with a No. 3 trap from Havahart Animal Traps, Ossining, NY, baited with sardines, dogfood or table scraps) and releasing the animal *many* miles away is more humane.

SAY, WHO'S THE LITTLE BO PEEP ??

Raccoons are highly susceptible to rabies, canine distemper, and several forms of encephalitis; these last two can be spread to dogs but not to people. They can also carry many bacterial diseases, including tuberculosis, listeriosis, and leptospirosis, which is a potential public health hazard in some areas.

If the above isn't enough to discourage you from keeping raccoons as pets, just remember that split personality. Besides tearing your furniture to ribbons, they will inevitably turn on you. Even city raccoons belong in the wild.

THE SKUNK
the nose knows

Size:	Between 2.2 and 3.5 kilograms for the striped skunk, and between 0.9 and 1.3 kilograms for the spotted skunk.
Colour:	Both species are black and white, though there are variations such as reddish brown, silver, and all black; albinos are common in striped but rare in spotted skunks; the striped skunk has a white stripe starting at the tip of a pointed noise that broadens down the back and goes to the tip of a bushy tail; the spotted skunk has six wavy white lines, often broken to form spots.
Range:	The striped skunk is found coast to coast south of the tree line, the spotted is found in the midwest and southeastern U.S.A.
Habitat:	Underground dens, under porches, almost anywhere in suburbia.
Food:	Omnivorous.
Breeding:	Each species has one litter per year, the striped has six to eight young per litter, while the spotted has three to five per litter.
Life Span:	Approximately four years.
Active:	They are nocturnal (the spotted more so than the striped) and they are not true hibernators.

When taxonomists dished out the latin names for our wildlife, they sure gave the skunks a smelly deal. The two common urban varieties, the striped and spotted skunks, are called *Mephitis mephitis* and *Spilogale putorius,* which mean "bad odour, bad odour" and "stinking spotted weasel," respectively. One author has described the striped skunk as a "fat, short-legged housecat." An adult male is about seventy-five centimeters long and weighs between 2.2 and 3.5 kilograms, but one chubby fellow reached a record 7.3 kilograms. The smaller, weasel-like spotted skunk is only about fifty centimeters long and weighs between 0.9 and 1.3 kilograms. Generally, males are 10 percent heavier than females.

The larger species' white stripe begins as a small strip at the tip of the nose and becomes a broad one on the crown of the head before branching at the shoulders and continuing to the tip of the tail. Variations abound, such as two stripes, no stripes, half stripes, and narrow and wide stripes. Again with many variations, the spotted skunk basically has six wavy white lines, often broken to form large spots. Albinism, common in striped skunks, is rare in this species. Other colour variations, especially in the striped skunk, include creamy, reddish-brown, silver, and even all black fur coats.

Overall, the spotted skunk is quicker and more nocturnal and alert than its larger cousin. Their finer and denser fur is often found about den entrances. With a good nose, one can distinguish the more pungent scent of the spotted skunk. Both species have five toes on their fore- and hindfeet (although the fifth toe is not always obvious in their tracks).

If you ever find yourself face to face with a skunk and have the presence of mind to do so, take a moment to notice its beady, black eyes; they contain no nictitating membrane (or third eyelid), which is unique among carnivores. Their canine teeth are razor sharp, and the nails on their forefeet, 2.5 centimeters long, are indicative of an excellent digging ability. Their hearing is average and their eyesight is poor beyond a range of eight meters. Skunks have a keen sense of smell, though, and they frequently clear their bulbous noses by sneezing.

Let's not forget the other business end of this animal. On each side of the anus there is a scent gland about 2.5 centimeters long, with a protruding nipple. Powerful sphincter muscles can force out either an atomized spray of almost invisible droplets or a short stream of rain-sized drops accurately up to three meters (but beware, it may still reach you at five meters). Through various body contortions, the nipples can be aimed behind, to either side of, or in front of the skunk's body to cover an angle of thirty to forty-five degrees. The secretion is not scattered with the tail, and if it's any comfort to you, no urine is released with the musk. The glands are good for about five to eight shots each, totalling roughly two tablespoons of musk. Replenishing a full load takes two days. More about skunk perfume later.

Few figures are available on skunk numbers, but a good estimate for dense populations (and cities certainly fall into this category) is one animal per four hectares. The striped skunk is found just about anywhere coast to coast south of the tree line in North America, whereas the spotted is mainly relegated to the midwestern and southeastern states.

Striped skunks are highly tolerant of other skunks in their home range because unlike their spotted cousin, which is more closely tied to a particular den, they are content to sleep anywhere dark and protected. Females might spend their entire lives in an area just over two hundred meters in diameter, whereas the larger male requires between two and two-and-a-half kilometers to range about in. During the breeding season, a male can clock up to eight kilometers per night while looking for a female.

CAN I KEEP THE KITTYCAT, DADDY ?? <u>HUH</u>, DADDY ??

For a striped skunk, the search for food usually entails a leisurely walk at 1.6 kilometers per hour, but they can trot at 5 and even gallop at 12 kilometers per hour. Over a short distance their top speed is 16 kilometers per hour, thus allowing humans to outrun them in the unlikely event of a chase. The spotted skunk is even slower, though it can climb trees, including jumping up and descending head first. The larger skunk can only negotiate wire mesh less than one meter high, but will win any aquatic race. Although both species swim infrequently, the spotted's limit is 180 meters, while one striped specimen swam for almost eight hours in water at 23° centigrade.

Being generally nocturnal, skunks begin foraging at sunset. With that black fur they especially avoid hot, sunny days. Some exceptions include newly weaned skunks, those searching for a mate on an overcast day during breeding season, and those hungry after a long period of winter denning. In areas where rabies is prevalent, a skunk wandering about in broad daylight is bad news.

During winter denning, skunks are not hibernating, they are merely lethargic. A rise in temperature will bring them out to hunt. This can be critical to an animal that can lose up to 65 percent of its body weight during those cold months.

You can get quite close to a skunk. However, at about four meters the following will occur: The skunk's fur will stand erect, inflating its size. The tail will be held high. Accompanying these will be the stamping of forefeet and maybe the clicking of teeth. If you step closer, the skunk will assume a U-shaped position with both its head and tail facing you. The spotted skunk is famous for its handstand act, whereby it walks for several meters on its forefeet, arching it back so as to aim its nipples towards the enemy's face. Some people contend that this pose serves only to enlarge the animal and hence frighten away any antagonist.

If the antagonist doesn't have the sense to leave after witnessing the above behavior, the skunk will unload its musk at a range of about 2.5 meters. The yellow to yellowish-green musk contains butylmercaptan, a chemical used in the development of mustard gas in World War I. Taken internally, this chemical can cause unconsciousness, lower body temperature, blood pressure and pulse, and depress the central nervous system. From a skunk, it only causes temporary blindness (for ten to fifteen minutes), perhaps nausea, and certainly injured pride. Just a few drops of the musk can saturate several square kilometers. Generally used for defense only, some people claim that skunks use minor doses to mark territorial boundaries and for communication during courtship.

Even courting skunks are not very vocal, but overall they are capable of growls, grunts, snarls, squeals, screeches, and churring and hissing noises. Injured individuals emit loud, high-pitched squeals. How's that for a repertoire?

Urbanized skunks readily den beneath houses, garages, outbuildings, culverts, and near dumps. The striped skunk, with its long nails, is quite capable of digging out a den. Most burrows are 1.8 to 6.1 meters long, about one meter below the surface and consist of one to five well-hidden entrances about twenty centimeters in diameter.

Since they might spend between seventy-five and a hundred straight days of winter in a den, dead grass and leaves are carried in for insulation. Generally communal, except for males with harems or females nursing young, a den might contain up to two dozen individuals in any combination of sex and age. They're not averse to curling up with raccoons and opossums for warmth; even rabbits and woodchucks are welcome guests.

Most skunks breed in March or April, but the western version of the spotted skunk produces its litter in late September. An adult male dens with his harem, fighting off other males. One fellow fertilized six den females and they all gave birth the same day. Coitus can be quite forceful and violent, with both partners biting and dragging one another around. Usually only one litter is produced (rarely, a striped female will raise two in one year). The larger skunk's litter size is between six and eight young (though eighteen is the record), while the spotted skunk has three to five (with a record of seven). By twenty-eight days of age, the young can discharge a small amount of musk. At six weeks, they will follow Mom in single file during foraging. By the next spring, they're ready to produce their own young.

Skunks are omnivorous and so eat just about anything edible they can catch. Like a cat, they either lie in wait or stalk their victims. Skunks will trap small prey with their forefeet, as well as dig small, conical holes in search of grubs and insects. They will even return to their own droppings to eat the beetles feeding on them. Although they have been known to prey upon half-grown kittens, skunks benefit mankind by feeding on mice, rats, and moles. Interestingly, skunks are clever enough to render some creatures harmless to them by rolling them across the ground; this removes poisonous bristles from fuzzy caterpillars, skin poison from toads, and expends the beetles' defensive secretions. Skunks also have a fondness for the larvae and honey of bees and suffer no ill effect from their stings. One skunk seemed hardly bothered by sixty-five stings in its mouth and throat.

Most experts agree that skunks are very lucky to see their fourth birthday in the wild. One captive reached ten years of age. It only takes five years to replace a given population. Body fat accumulation has a lot to do with their life expectancy. If they're forced to retire to their winter dens earlier than usual or remain in them for prolonged periods during winter, skunks, especially juveniles, simply die of starvation. House cats occasionally kill spotted skunks, and some dogs, after being sprayed, become persistent skunk killers. Great horned owls, who are often found nesting in urban ravines and who are resistant to skunk musk, relish skunk dinners. One owl nest had fifty-seven carcasses below it.

How often does one see a battered skunk carcass lying on the road? Oddly, they're mostly striped skunks. Possibly spotted ones either back away from car headlights or refrain from foraging along roads.

Skunks are susceptible to many diseases, but two—leptospirosis and rabies—are noteworthy. Leptospirosis, the most widespread disease among animals, is prevalent wherever you find infected animals, urine, water, and humans together. The bacteria shed by animals enter humans through abrasions and cuts in the skin and through intact membranes of the eyes, nose and mouth, resulting in fever, muscular pains and jaundice. Rabies is transmitted to humans via a virus in the skunk's saliva delivered during a bite. Of the two kinds of rabies, the "dumb" type does not cause the viciousness or desire to roam as seen in the "furious" strain. The incidence of the virus varies yearly, but is quite prevalent in the range of the striped skunk. In 1977, for example, 60 percent of all cases of rabies in wildlife was attributed to skunks. Apparently the disease may be transmitted among skunks during copulation, when the animals tend to bite one another.

Well, to say that skunks are all right as long as people leave them alone would be dishonest. True, they do gobble up a lot of injurious pests (only 5 percent of their diet is economically valuable to people), but occasionally they can be a nuisance. For example, they uproot cabbages in their search for June bugs, which eat—you guessed it—cabbages. Like squirrels, woodchucks and raccoons, these critters enjoy feeding on your backyard corn, but a fence one meter high and fifteen centimeters below the surface and fifteen centimeters horizontally (L-shaped to prevent digging) will keep them out. Skunks also dig conical holes ranging in size from seven to ten centimeters in lawns. However, if one eradicates the grubs and insects they're looking for, the problem is eliminated. If keeping bees is your hobby in suburbia, raising the hives about one meter will minimize skunks getting at them. As with all

"WILD KINGDOM" IS THEIR FAVORITE SHOW!

city critters, tightly fitting lids on garbage cans, or pouring bleach, Lysol, ammonia or motor oil on your garbage, preclude cleaning up any mess a skunk can make.

Even the issue of skunks being carriers of disease pales in comparison to the reaction to their odour. In short, some people just don't care to share their homes with skunks. If you've got a skunk or two or three living under your house or garage, the best approach is to seal off all the entrances but one, sprinkle a fine layer of flour around the opening, and examine it after sunset. If the animal has left, seal it off. If you're unsure as to how many skunks there are in the den, or if there is a litter (from early May to mid-August), a door of 13 mm wire mesh that opens only outwards will allow them to leave. Sealing up any animal in its den to die of starvation is not only cruel, but will likely create an even greater odour problem. The same goes for skunks entering garages, basements, and so on; just open the door and let them vacate the premises at their own leisure. For those trapped in window wells, a helping hand in the form of a gangplank would be courteous.

Some experts advocate the use of mothballs or napthalene crystals to repel skunks from unwanted spaces. For burrows, 450 grams are recommended, but five to ten times as much is needed for attics and crawlspaces. It should be placed on a shallow tray for easy removal or hung out of reach of children and pets in coarse-mesh cloth sacks, and must be replaced often. Lysol- or ammonia-soaked rags are supposedly a turn-off for skunks as well. If you overdo it, though, you may burn the animal. This tactic should not be used on skunk litters, as the young will die before the mother can move them.

OK, you've tried all of the above and they didn't work, so what next? It just so happens that skunks are very easy to live-trap, and if they're released ten kilometers away (preferably not near other homes), they won't return. Fish, fishy cat food, raw or cooked bacon, peanut butter, chicken parts, or combinations of the above are excellent bait items. But even if you approach the trap gently and darken it with a tarp or burlap, there's no guarantee you won't get sprayed. Skunks will avoid spraying themselves though, so holding their tails over their anus or pushing their rears against the ground will curtail any musk release. In fact, both biting and spraying can be minimized by grasping the animal around the neck with one hand and by the tail with the other. The skunk should be turned on its back with the tail pointed away and downwind. One thing is certain: skunks can spray while suspended by their tail.

Pets or humans can be deodorized by saturating them in tomato juice, turpentine, or vinegar, followed by a good bath. Especially effective is a deodorant agent called neutroleum alpha, which is available from hospital-supply houses or pest-control operators. A solution of this chemical can also be used to scrub the smell from basements, garages, floors, and walls, or to soak contaminated soil. If blasted in the face by a skunk, the stinging and temporary blindness can be overcome more quickly by rinsing the eyes with water. Sprayed clothes are not a write-off, either; washing them several times with soap or detergent combined with household ammonia will do the trick.

Lastly, a comment on skunks as pets. Spotted skunks are excitable and not easily tamed, but de-scented striped ones are docile enough to be house pets. However, aside from any legal considerations, any skunk, if kept too long, will become a nuisance by chewing on valuable objects. As time goes on, they will show less congeniality as well. Without scent glands, a skunk cannot be released into the wild. Hence, you're condemning it to death row. They are better off left in the wild.

THE COTTONTAIL
rabbits, rabbits everywhere

Size:	800 to 1800 grams.
Colour:	Gray, brownish-gray; very rarely albino, white, buff, and black cottontails are seen.
Range:	East of the Rockies in the U.S. and in southern Canada.
Habitat:	Areas heavily planted with low vegetation, thickets; dens and burrows dug by skunks and woodchucks.
Food:	Bluegrass, red clover, woody plants, bark, dandelions, ragweed, peas, carrots, beans, lettuce, cabbage, and flowers.
Breeding:	Three litters per year in the north, six litters per year in the south, each containing three to six young.
Life Span:	15 months.
Active:	During the night; they are not true hibernators.

Very few suburban residents can say they've never seen a rabbit during early evening or morning in their neck of the woods. Almost certainly, that rabbit was an eastern cottontail; they're found all over the U.S.A. east of the Rockies and in southern parts of Canada—essentially anywhere where there's food and cover for them.

Cottontails thrive in towns and cities, frequenting vacant lots, gardens, shrub plantings, golf courses, parks, and heavily planted residential areas. They particularly like thickets of blackberries and rose plants of various species.

A true rabbit (defined by its mostly naked young, which are helpless at birth), the cottontail is generally gray or brownish-gray and derives its name from that cottonball of a tail. Very rarely, true albinos, white, buff and black individuals show up. Although they molt their fur twice annually, the colour stays the same year-round. The sexes are similarly coloured, but females tend to be slightly larger than males. Overall, their size ranges from eight hundred to eighteen hundred grams. It is their deeply cleft upper lip that has given rise to the expression "hare lipped." By the way, that nose only twitches because of the transverse chewing motion of the rabbit's jaws.

Cottontails do not maintain territories, but home ranges comprise anywhere between .2 and 16 hectares. Perhaps a decent estimate might be one rabbit per .4 hectare. They do, however, move around occasionally for food. A given rabbit could spend its entire life within an area of four hectares. For efficiency in foraging and evading enemies, cottontails use paths, trails and even roads. They're fairly quick, too, covering up to four and a half meters in the first few leaps and maintaining a speed of roughly 30 kilometers per hour in short springs. Cottontails often zig-zag, double back, and sometimes squat and freeze to avoid detection.

Just around dawn and at sunset are good times to spot these rabbits because they are basically nocturnal. Lawns, mowed areas, cemeteries, golf courses—anywhere with low vegetation—are prime locations. Don't bother to look for them during storms, heavy snowfall or sudden drops in temperature. Don't expect to hear them either, as cottontails are generally silent. Soft grunting sounds are made by nursing mothers, and the thumping of hindfeet is a warning of danger. One apparently unforgettable sound, however, is the shrill, high-pitched scream of a rabbit in serious trouble.

To avoid inclement weather or to escape enemies, they use burrows excavated by skunks and woodchucks (they do not, as is popularly believed, dig their own), or seek cover in and under rock crevices, cavities in stumps, old rolls of fence wire, junked car parts, drainage pipes and tiles, small culverts, and stacks of lumber and steel pipe. They do not appear to be a major problem under building foundations.

During the day in spring or fall, these rabbits might either sunbathe or seek shade in a "form." These shallow nests are merely slanted holes between nine and eleven centimeters deep and measuring fifteen centimeters long by eleven wide. Dug by the females, sometimes right out in the open on lawns, they're lined with grass and with fur plucked from anywhere but the abdomen.

The cottontail's breeding season extends anywhere from the first week in January in the south to the last week in March in the north. (In Texas they breed year-round.) Cottontails are promiscuous and the females are induced ovulators, that is ovulation only occurs after copulation or other suitable stimuli. The courtship is brief, consisting of a quick chase, head-to-head encounters, and lively hops over one another just prior to the actual act, which lasts from one to four seconds. The expression "breeding like a rabbit" does have some basis in fact. With up to three litters per year in the north, and as many as six in the south, each of which contains between three and six

young, it's not surprising that some females produce up to twenty-nine young every year. The gestation period is only twenty-eight or twenty-nine days, and within a few hours of giving birth, the female is ready to start all over again.

Essentially naked except for some very fine gray fur, the young are about ten centimeters long and weigh about thirty grams. Their eyes open after about six or eight days. After two or three weeks, they leave the nest and are ready to produce their own young. The female cottontail nurses her young with milk that is four times richer than the average cow's.

The high reproductive rate is offset by a correspondingly heavy mortality rate. Some researchers say that 44 percent of the newborn die within a month. Maybe one in one hundred makes it to the autumn. Certainly many don't live past fifteen months, though one wild individual was recorded at five years of age, and captives have lived for ten years.

Heavy rains can wash out some nests. Vehicles take their toll as well, particularly during March and April when the breeding season starts. Occasionally, young rabbits become trapped in window wells. Even in urban areas, predators probably account for most cottontail deaths. Raccoons, skunks, snakes, hawks, and owls readily take both adults and young. Dogs and cats kill their fair share, too. Even crows have been observed preying upon young rabbits.

Cottontails munch on herbaceous species (especially bluegrass and red clover) in the growing season, and woody plants (especially apple, red maple, blackberry, raspberry and staghorn sumac) in the dormant season. They do not dig for bulbs or roots, but will dig in deep snow for frozen apples if all else fails, including eating their own feces. Two types of pellets are excreted; a hard brown one containing 60 percent nutrients, and a soft green pellet. The latter contains vitamin B and is eaten directly from the anus. Lastly, cottontails have been observed licking paved roads, presumably for the salt put there in the winter time.

Well, the good news is that young cottontails eat dandelions and ragweed. The bad news is that they also eat garden vegetables and damage flowers and woody plants. They especially like the first tulip shoots of spring. Peas, carrots, beans, lettuce, and cabbage are among their garden favourites, so I recommend you grow cucumbers, corn, squash, tomatoes, peppers and potatoes. Or build a fence. A wire fence of 2.5 cm diameter mesh that is 1.6 meters high and buried a dozen centimeters below the surface will do the trick. Napthalene mothballs or dried blood meal (available from plant nurseries) have been

HERE'S TWO BUCKS, BUT I'VE NEVER HEARD OF
ANY "EASTER BUNNY PENSION FUND" BEFORE!

used with some success as repellents in small gardens, but the latter must be replenished after any rain.

Gnawing the bark and nipping off the branches, stems and buds of ornamental trees and shrubs are also major problems with cottontails in urban areas. The smooth bark underlaid with juicy green material is delicious food to rabbits, while they ignore thick, rough bark. Apple trees, and raspberry and blackberry bushes are the most frequently damaged, but cherry, plum and nut trees fall victim to rabbits as well. Occasionally evergreens, particularly pines, are selected.

Commercial tree wrap is available, but you can use .6 cm wire hardware cloth (which also keeps out mice) installed to at least above the height of a rabbit stretching on its hind legs on snow cover. If you use 1.3 or 1.9 cm cloth, it must be kept away from the trunk to prevent the rabbits from eating through the wire. Taste repellents are also available, but they have their drawbacks in that they must be replaced after heavy rains and do not protect new growth.

As long as your neighbours agree, modifying the environment is one answer. You'll have to remove piles of brush and debris, and it doesn't hurt to have a few trees around to encourage the rabbits' natural enemies—raccoons, hawks, and owls. Some people have advocated leaving out a piece of rubber hose (which apparently looks like a snake to the rabbit) or a large, clear glass jar of water (distortion supposedly terrifies them), but I'd be surprised if these methods really worked. Lastly, cottontails can be live-trapped with ease by placing a homemade box trap baited with dried apple, carrot or cabbage near a runway. A word of caution: rabbits can inflict deep scratches and deliver hard blows with their hind feet. They should be released several kilometers away and not near other people's homes.

If a rabbit appears sluggish and tame, the local authorities should be notified immediately. Although not very common, in some states, 90 percent of all cases of tularemia in humans is attributable to rabbits. This plague-like bacterial disease can be contracted by direct contact with the flesh or blood of, or by eating infected rabbits. White spots on the liver and spleen of the animal are indicative of the disease. The carcass should be burned, hands washed and disinfected, and cuts or abrasions treated with iodine. Tularemia is fatal to the rabbit and is prevalent in spring and fall.

Many of the ticks carried by rabbits are transmissible to humans and domestic pets; Rocky Mountain spotted fever is spread by tick bites.

All things considered, cottontails are best left to their rather hectic lives in the wild. Like any wild animal, they soon outlive both their novelty and their congeniality as pets. (Besides, domestic rabbits are readily available for this purpose.) Actually, the number of wild rabbits has declined in the last fifty years. They're simply running out of food and places to hide. Hence, urban habitats have become an important resource for this animal.

Presuming that you do want them around your backyard, I recommend supplemental feeding, such as prunings (especially honeysuckle) and waste corn. A salt lick isn't a bad idea, either. As for cover, brushpiles four to six meters in diameter and one to two meters high placed along fencerows and hedges are welcomed by rabbits. For something a little more aesthetic, however, natural thorny shrubs or low, dense clump-type growth such as ornamentals are ideal. Enclosing window wells with transparent domes or installing ramps will prevent needless deaths.

One last comment. A little tête-à-tête with your neighbours prior to implementing your plans to boost the local rabbit population might help avert World War Three.

OPOSSUMS
the great pretenders

Size:	Three to six kilograms.
Colour:	Usually gray, but variations include blackish, cinnamon coloured, albino, and white; the opossum is a marsupial (bearing its young in a pouch), with a long pointy face, round hairless ears, and a hairless tail.
Range:	Southern Ontario and British Columbia, and most of the southern U.S.A. east of the Rockies.
Habitat:	Under trees, culverts, attics, garages building foundations; among rocks; dens dug by skunks and woodchucks.
Food:	Almost anything edible, including poisonous snakes like copperheads and rattlesnakes, as well as earthworms, insects, carrion, apples, and other opossums.
Breeding:	Two litters per year each containing seven or eight young.
Life Span:	About three years.
Active:	They are nocturnal.

To paraphrase Captain John Smith's words, spoken in 1612, the opossum has the head of a pig, the tail of a rat, and is the size of a cat. Not a bad description considering the opossum's long pointed face, round hairless ears, and rat-like tail that is just less than half its total body length. The most common colour is gray, but blackish individuals occur in the gulf coastal states. Other variations include cinnamon, true albinos, and white opossums.

The opossum has fifty teeth, more than any other North American mammal. This creature has one more distinction: although it is not a holdover from the dinosaurs as is commonly believed, the opossum is the only marsupial (bearing its young in a pouch) on the continent.

Another myth is their so-called slow-wittedness. Far from stupid, opossums have ranked above the dog and rivalled the pig in intelligence tests. Their powers of smell and touch are well-developed, but their hearing is not especially keen. They appear to be myopic, but do see in colour.

Due to their ability to store large amounts of fat, some old animals can weigh up to 13.5 kilograms, but the heaviest wild male was recorded at 5.9 kilograms. The average male and female weights are three and six kilograms, respectively. If you really want to determine the sex of an individual, you can't avoid examining at least one of their two business ends. The females have pouches, while males have scrotums and consistently larger and heavier canines.

Opossums are found in southern Ontario and British Columbia, as well as over most of the U.S.A., except the Rockies, some western plains states, and some northern parts. Climate and the availability of den sites and winter food limit their range.

Information on their numbers is very sparse. The sex ratio at birth is equal, but after weaning, males appear to predominate. Home ranges are also difficult to determine. Opossums are not territorial, do not maintain separate home ranges, and some individuals are very nomadic. A rough approximation though, might be four opossums to twenty hectares. Young males wander more widely than females. Among other examples, one mother carried her ten pouched young over thirty-five hundred meters in four days. Home ranges must contain a number of suitable dens, as well as access to water.

An opossum walks at between .48 and 1.6 kilometers per hour, but it can move as quickly as 7.4 kilometers per hour. They're not especially rapid or agile climbers in spite of having an opposable thumb and a prehensile tail that acts as a fifth leg. They can indeed hang by that tail. Opossums are not bad swimmers, either, being able to paddle about one hundred meters on the surface and six meters underwater, with their eyes open.

They make four distinct sounds: hissing, growling, screeching, and "clicking." This last one has a metallic ring, and is probably made by clashing the canines together.

Being shy and nocturnal, opossums are seldom seen. However, they're occasionally observed in the daytime during warm spells in winter.

Although a ploy not unique to them, feigning death when faced with an inescapable threat is common to 'possums. They will fall on their side with the body slightly flexed, the eyes opened, the corners of the mouth drawn back, the jaws opened somewhat, and drooling saliva. They also expel a greenish, foul-smelling substance from their anal glands. This behavior can also occur when a wild opossum is caught by hand.

Interestingly opossums are highly resistant to the venom of rattlesnakes, cottonmouths and copperheads, and because they eat just about anything edible under the

UH...I THINK I'LL TAKE THIS ONE.

sun, snakes are part of the opossum's diet. These oppor-
tunistic critters eat whatever is abundant. Besides preying
upon a number of vertebrates and invertebrates (especially
earthworms and insects), opossums eat vegetation
(especially persimmons and apples), scavenge for carrion
and garbage, and cannibalize smaller, weaker individuals.

Opossums are incapable of digging their own burrows,
and so depend on those dug by skunks and woodchucks.
Other dens include holes, cracks, and crevices in and under
trees, stumps, hollow logs, vine tangles, road culverts,
attics, garages, building foundations, drainage tiles, piles
of brush, rock and debris, and even garbage cans.
Opossums will enlarge the arboreal nests of wood rats,
crows and squirrels by adding grass and leaves transported
in their coiled tails. One thing is certain—their dens are
always within three hundred meters of water. Surprisingly,
the omnivorous opossum will share its dens with skunks,
raccoons, woodchucks, cottontail rabbits, shrews, mice,
weasels, snakes, and invertebrates.

The reproductive season begins in January and extends
to the weaning of the last litter in November. Upon
finding an estrous female, the male chases her about,
"clicking" continually. Copulation lasts about twenty
minutes, but notably, the mating pair tumble over on
their right sides to achieve sperm transfer (the left side

apparently doesn't work). An opossum definitely does not
copulate with his mate's nose, as is commonly believed.

The gestation period lasts twelve days and eighteen hours,
and once labour begins the young are expelled within
twelve minutes. The tiny opossums, weighing .13 grams
and about the size of a honeybee, climb up to fifty
millimeters to the pouch, where they either attach
themselves to a nipple or die. This, of course, determines
the litter size, which generally consists of seven or eight
young, but has been as high as twenty-one. Although
some experts claim that opossums can have three litters
a year, most females have only two.

The female does not pump milk into the attached young,
nor is there any fusion of lips and tongue to the nipple
as once believed. The female needs the stimulus of at least
two suckling young to produce milk. All she really does
beyond that is clean both the pouch and her young. The
babies are attached to the teats for up to eight weeks,
and finally wean themselves after about seven more weeks
of maternal care. Not all of them fit in the pouch, so some
cling to the fur on the mother's back. Five to six months
later, they're capable of producing their own young.

While most wild opossums probably do not live beyond
three years of age, a maximum of seven has been attained.
A population can turn over in three and a half years, as

most of the young die in their first year. After severe winters, many of them are marked by excessive numbers of cuts, scratches, ripped ears, lost toes, and broken teeth and bones. Frostbite accounts for the missing parts of tails or ears seen on some individuals. Opossums are noted for how quickly any wounds they suffer will heal.

Opossums are preyed upon by various carnivores, but dogs and great horned owls are significant predators in urban areas. Since they feed readily upon roadkills, many opossums lose their lives to cars.

Opossums harbour heavy loads of many varieties of parasites, but cat fleas and dog ticks number among the greatest of these. Although opossums are hardly noticed in urban habitats, they do make occasional visits to food dishes intended for pets, birdfeeders, backyard gardens, and garbage cans. They can also make messy nests in attics, garages, and under building foundations. While some precautions have been described elsewhere in this book, like tight-fitting garbage can lids, the installation of a tightly stretched electrified wire near the top of a fence, 7.6 centimeters out from the mesh will keep them out. Opossums are also easily live-trapped. Baiting with cheese, fish, or slightly spoiled food is effective, but using fruit will lessen the chance of catching skunks or pets in your trap. Opossums should be released several kilometers away.

To some people these strange animals may be less than attractive, but they sure as heck are interesting enough to be left alone!

THE WOODCHUCK
how much ground can a groundhog hog?

Size:	Between 2.3 and 5.4 kilograms.
Colour:	Grizzled brownish gray, tinged with red; rarely are albino or black woodchucks seen; the eyes and ears of the woodchuck are located on top of the head.
Range:	Eastern U.S.A. and southern Canada.
Habitat:	Digs burrows and tunnels.
Food:	Vegetables, grasses, legumes, and fruit trees.
Breeding:	One litter per year of four or five young.
Life Span:	Four years.
Active:	In the early morning and evening when it's hot, midday during the spring and fall, they are true hibernators.

The woodchuck (or groundhog, as some people call it) deserves a few words. Sure, I know they prefer open farmland, but I also know I've seen them in golf courses, parks, ravines, and big backyards in suburban areas. Woodchucks can be found from Labrador and Nova Scotia across the southern half of Canada, north to southeastern Alaska and over most of the eastern half of the U.S.A.

The largest member of the squirrel family, woodchucks may weigh up to 6.8 kilograms, but generally range from 2.3 to 5.4 kilograms in size. The sexes are similar in appearance, though males are slightly larger. Rarely will you see an albino or black individual.

Their eyes, ears and nose are located on the top of the head to facilitate peering over the rim of their burrows at potential threats. They also have three anal glands, but the musk is not nearly as powerful as that of you-know-who. Woodchucks are quite clean and will actually deposit their feces in special dead-end chambers where they are partially buried.

Digging out over three hundred kilograms of soil, the groundhog excavates some fifteen to eighteen meters of tunnels as deep as five meters. The single burrow may have five entrances. A main entrance is usually located beneath a tree stump, stone wall, or among rocks, while the plunge hole, with a vertical drop of about sixty centimeters, is dug from within so as to leave no dirt around for detection. Evidence of woodchuck residences consists of well-kept surface trails and freshly worked dirt piles. Their entire lives are probably restricted to within three hundred meters of the den, though many groundhogs seldom wander beyond even a hundred meters of it.

Woodchucks can gallop as fast as 16 kilometers per hour and, surprisingly, can swim quite well with just their noses and tops of their heads above the surface. They can also forage in trees. One startled chuck zipped five meters up a jack pine, while others have been seen sitting around nine meters up in trees. They emit a loud, shrill whistle just before diving to safety. Cornered individuals will grind their teeth while chattering; a handled animal might issue a muffled bark.

On hot summer days, their preferred feeding times are early morning and evening; midday is favoured during the cooler times of spring and autumn. They don't like rainy weather. When not feeding their faces, woodchucks often squat in the mouths of their dens, sunning, preening, scratching, and pulling their fur.

Unlike many other four-legged mammals in North America, woodchucks do undergo true hibernation by entering torpor. Their heartbeat drops from one hundred beats per minute to about fifteen, the body temperature from 35° centigrade to 8° and their breathing rate decreases to less than one inhalation per six minutes.

This is like telling children there's no Santa Claus, but Groundhog Day has no factual basis whatsoever. Woodchucks often emerge during spells of warm weather, even in mid-winter.

Being vegetarians, groundhogs eat a variety of vegetables, grasses and legumes. Rarely do they eat insects, snails or birds' eggs. They especially relish beans, peas, carrot tops, alfalfa, clover and grasses; they can put away .67 kilograms of food daily.

Reproduction carries on from early March to late April. Woodchucks only have one litter annually and the number of young ranges from two to nine, but most often is four or five. Able to crawl at three weeks, they become full-fledged junior woodchucks at six weeks of age. They can breed in their first year, but often wait until their second year. That's unfortunate for the woodchuck because they

HOW IS HE SUPPOSED TO <u>SEE</u> HIS SHADOW, ANYWAY??

seldom live beyond four years of age, though there are records of six-year-olds, and captive animals have lived for ten years.

Flooding and heavy rains drown some woodchucks in their burrows and a good number die as roadkills each year. Interestingly, as a result of overgrown incisors, some die from starvation or from the teeth actually penetrating their skulls.

Woodchucks generally flee into their burrows to escape predation, but they can be fierce fighters if cornered. That doesn't prevent dogs from killing them in suburban areas.

The woodchuck's two greatest loves, eating and burrowing, are what puts it in direct conflict with people. Groundhogs can clean out a backyard garden of peas, beans or squash in a matter of hours, especially with the help of four or five growing youngsters. Fruit trees and ornamental shrubs are also damaged by their gnawing and clawing. Some homeowners object strongly to the extensive burrowing under the foundations of their houses. Occasional digging on golf-course fairways may also be bothersome.

Since the woodchuck is a good climber, the only fence that will keep them out extends at least a hundred centimeters above the ground and about thirty centimeters below it. But that's not all—an electric hot-shot wire between ten and thirteen centimeters off the ground and outside the fence is a must. Minimizing their security by mowing a good distance around your garden's edge and ridding your backyard of cover in the form of brush piles and tall grasses just might (I said *might*) dissuade woodchucks from homesteading on your property.

They can be live-trapped by placing a trap near the burrow entrance or on a runway. There is some controversy as to how difficult this is. If you don't have a garden and don't mind sharing some underground turf, woodchucks can be very interesting tenants. Their burrows also provide homes for raccoons, opossums, and skunks. Believe it or not, the growth of your vegetation, including trees, can be enhanced by the added fertilization from the groundhogs' buried fecal matter.

So how much ground can a groundhog hog? Just enough to be left alone to feed, breed, and watch the world go by.

THE POCKET GOPHER
a pox on gardens

Size:	Up to 200 grams.
Colour:	Pale brown back with gray sides; they have prominent incisors that protrude from the mouth and that must be worn down constantly.
Range:	Southern and western North America.
Habitat:	Digs burrows with tunnel systems in open areas with loose soil.
Food:	Leaves, roots, dandelions, goldenrod, bark, and vegetables.
Breeding:	One litter per year containing between one and eight young.
Life Span:	Three to four years.
Active:	Around the clock all year round.

Restricted to southern and western North America, particularly the plains and prairies, pocket gophers might be encountered any place where there's loose, soft soil and plenty of juicy, edible plants to munch on. They're only about twenty-three centimeters long and weigh up to two hundred grams (roughly three times larger than a mole). Pocket gophers are best known for the fur-lined cheek pouches that open on the outside of the face (not the inside of the mouth like chipmunks and squirrels) and are large enough to accommodate a thumb or index finger.

Gophers have large, prominent incisor teeth that protrude from the front of the mouth; they minimize the dirt eaten while cutting apart roots. The lower incisors grow at a rate of .099 millimeters per day, and if they aren't constantly worn down by the gopher's gnawing, they can reach a length of 3.5 centimeters in one year.

Besides being active around the clock, pocket gophers are also about year-round. They even burrow quite freely through deep snow to find food in winter. The gopher's

WHEN I SAID I NEEDED SOME "GOFERS" AROUND THE OFFICE, I DIDN'T MEAN···

tunnel system generally consists of deep galleries and shallow feeding tunnels. Sometimes as deep as 2.7 meters, they average about 1.8 meters; they are usually below the frostline. One excavated deep tunnel was fifty meters long. Apparently, gophers can run backwards through their burrows, using their sensitive tails as probes. Except during the mating season, they're not likely to run into each other because these quarrelsome critters will even plug connecting tunnels to avoid meeting one another.

During the breeding season in May, males will enter the burrows of females, and about twenty days later, there are a few more gophers in the world, somewhere between one and eight per litter.

Even though gophers have a keen sense of smell and decent hearing, they don't see very well. Gophers can be vicious fighters if cornered, but their life expectancy is only three or four years because a fair number fall prey to both winged and ground predators, especially skunks, snakes, owls, dogs, and cats.

Leaves supply about 70 percent of their food, and roots the other 30. While the stems and leaves of plants might be taken during nocturnal forays, gophers are famous for burrowing under plants, cutting their roots, and yanking them into the burrow from below. The good news is that they will eat dandelions and goldenrod. The bad news is that they're also partial to potatoes, carrots, parsnips, artichokes, turnips, beets, radishes, peas, beans, and ornamental plants. Occasionally, when other food is scarce, gophers will kill young trees by eating the bark all around the trunks.

I wouldn't wish a gopher on anyone's backyard because they usually come in bunches. You can tell if they're around; besides a number of missing plants, you'll notice mounds containing between two liters and a bushel of dirt. Unlike the mole, the gopher pushes the soil out from the entrance in a fan-shaped configuration, blocking the entrance with a firm earth plug. They also don't leave a raised ridge in the turf the way moles do, but their mounds can wreak havoc with a power lawnmower.

Gophers don't like underground power and telephone cables blocking their way, so they simply gnaw through any lead and copper sheeting, thereby shorting the wires out. Installing the cables with a hard metal jacketing in the first place will avert this problem.

There is no nice, easy way to rid your backyard of the pocket gopher. If you can live with losing a few, well, maybe a lot, of your garden produce and are willing to forego competing with the neighbours for the best lawn on the block, why not just enjoy these interesting subterranean critters.

THE MOLE
a tiny miner with a mountainous appetite

Size:	Between 85 and 115 grams.
Colour:	Greyish brown; moles have long naked snouts, large broad forefeet, and very small eyes.
Range:	Eastern U.S.A., southern Ontario.
Habitat:	Digs burrows with extensive tunnel systems in loamy, well-drained soil.
Food:	Earth worms, white grubs, insect larvae, insects, bulbs, and roots.
Breeding:	One litter per year containing between two and five young.
Life Span:	Not well-studied.
Active:	Day and night, all year round.

You may never see a mole, but if you do, you'll recognize it by its long, naked snout that extends 12.7 millimeters beyond its mouth, large broad forefeet, soft, velvety fur, and eyeballs reduced in size to the point of being almost useless. Their sense of smell is poor, but their hearing is well developed, though the degree of acuteness is not known. The mole's tactile ability is exceptional, and its sensitive nose is kept clean with frequent washings.

The eastern mole, the most common invader of urban areas, is found throughout the eastern half of the U.S. as well as parts of southern Ontario. It prefers soil where burrowing is easy, that is soil without a heavy clay or stony composition. Also important is soil moisture, but most crucial, of course, is the presence of food. Moles dine on earthworms, white grubs, insect larvae, adult insects, and vegetable matter; likely in that order, too. They have insatiable appetites and will often eat between 50 and 100 percent of their body weight daily. Moles need all that energy to accomplish the burrowing they do each day.

Moles burrow at 4.5 meters per hour with a unique lateral and alternating stroke; one mole dug thirty-one meters

of tunnel in one day. Another enterprising creature constructed thirty-two mounds (or molehills) in seventy-seven days. Both surface and deep tunnels are dug, and they become major thoroughfares for all kinds of tiny vertebrates and invertebrates. The urbanized mole makes its headquarters under buildings and sidewalks.

Molehills can easily be distinguished from gopher mounds by the former's volcano-like shape and the latter's fan-like configuration. The gopher's burrow entrance is marked by a plug of dirt, where the mole burrow is not. One final comparison is that the mole's home range is almost twenty times that of the pocket gopher.

The mole breeds but once a year, producing a litter of between two and five young. Little is known of their life span. Flooding is probably their greatest enemy, but a number fall prey to hawks, owls, snakes, raccoons, skunks, dogs and cats. One mole invaded an underground nest of yellow jackets and was stung to death for its effort.

Besides the occasional disfiguration of lawns and golf courses, moles can be indirectly responsible for damage to backyard gardens by dessicating the underground portions, such as the bulbs and roots of plants. In other words, any direct injury to plant material is confined strictly to the underground parts. There are no visible incisor tooth marks or angular stem clippings, as seen in gopher damage. Often, mice using the mole's tunnels are to blame for actually destroying your plants.

The damage to lawns, golf courses and flower beds must surely be offset by the mole's destruction of harmful insects. One inspired mole extended its molehill up to a low-hanging hornet's nest and ate all the young there. Moles also till and form the soil, permitting air and moisture to penetrate to the deeper levels. Sure, the earthworms gobbled up by moles are good at this, too, but everything in nature has its checks and balances.

Let's say you've got a problem though, and the mole has just got to go. There are many nasty ways to get rid of a mole, but you can catch it alive for release elsewhere by approaching it quietly on some fresh burrowing in the early morning or evening and using a spade to flip the little fellow up on the grass. Sometimes a stream of water from a hose or ditch directed into its burrow will cause it to surface. A pit trap using a large coffee can or wide glass jar buried mouth-up in the tunnel floor apparently works. A board placed above the trap will keep out the light, and the tunnel should be caved in on both sides so that the mole, unable to see the trap, will dig through and fall into the jar or can. Because of the mole's voracious appetite, the trap should be checked several times daily to avoid starving it to death.

I could tell you about a few remedies based on noise or vibrations, but I won't waste your time because they don't work. These include mole wheels, windmills, bleach bottles with wind vents on sticks, and pop bottles. As yet, there is no scientific proof that the planting of caper spurge or castor bean works, either. If you've really got a serious problem with moles, then forget the moles and rid your lawn of the white grubs they're feeding on.

All the same, moles are very intriguing neighbours and they are certainly worthy of a closer look.

THE HOUSE MOUSE
tiny and troublesome

Size: 11 to 22 grams.
Colour: Grayish brown.
Range: All over North America.
Habitat: Man-made structures, stored food, and burrows.
Food: Omnivorous, but prefer cereal grains.
Breeding: Eight litters per year each containing between four and seven young.
Life Span: One year.
Active: Nocturnal; all year round.

Second perhaps only to the Norway rat, the ubiquitous house mouse is the most troublesome and economically important rodent in North America. It is certainly the most common mammal in our cities, next to us, and is more common in residences and commercial structures than rats.

Requiring little or no water, these tiny omnivores prefer cereal grains. Mice are categorized as "nibblers" because they spoil more food by contamination than they eat; they eat about three grams daily.

House mice nest within structures and stored food, but will also dig burrows. Their average home range is between three and ten meters, and even in search of food, an individual will seldom travel beyond a hundred meters.

With a year-round breeding season, a nineteen-day gestation period, an average of eight litters per year—consisting of four to seven young—and an age at first breeding of about two months, we must be grateful that mice have an average life span of only one year.

This nocturnal "mighty mouse" can climb just about anywhere in any direction on any rough surface. It can also chew through wood, concrete, vinyl, rubber, and even aluminum. Few households are not homes to them, but you can make sure by looking for these signs: droppings, tracks, urine stains, smudge marks (from rubbing body oil on objects during constant passing), gnawing, various noises, odours, nests, and finally, direct sightings at night with a flashlight.

To minimize making life easy for them, household foods, pet foods and birdseed should be stored in mouse-proof containers. Large quantities of dry pet foods and birdseed can be nicely stored in metal garbage cans with tight-fitting lids. Leaving food in your pet's dish for long periods of time is not recommended.

The best way to avoid problems with infestations of house mice is simply to keep them out in the first place. Any hole or opening from the outside that is six millimeters or larger in diameter should be sealed with concrete mortar, sheet metal or heavy gauge hardware cloth.

While backyard wildlife can make life interesting for city folk, little can be said for encouraging numbers of the house mouse. It really needs little help. But during our sometimes futile efforts to control house mouse populations, we should keep in mind the enormous contributions to science and medicine made by its laboratory version.

– THE RAT
king of the underworld

Size:	The Norway rat weighs over 400 grams; the roof rat weighs between 150 and 250 grams.
Colour:	The Norway rat is brown with scattered black and has a yellowish white underbelly, the roof rat is brownish gray streaked with gray, gray, or black, and has a white, gray or black underbelly; the Norway rat has a shaggy coat, while the roof rat's is smooth.
Range:	The Norway rat is found across North America, while the roof rat is found on the southeastern coast, the gulf states, and the western coast.
Habitat:	Wherever humans live.
Food:	Both are relatively omnivorous; the roof rat eats fruit, nuts, grains, and vegetables; the Norway rat eats what is considered to be a well-balanced human diet; they both absolutely require water.
Breeding:	Both species have between four and seven litters per year; there are between eight and twelve young in a litter of Norway rats, and between four and eight young in a litter of roof rats.
Life Span:	One year for both species.
Active:	At night all year round.

I would be remiss if I failed to include in this book the undisputed king (the house mouse is the crown prince) of all city critters: the rat. While the Norway rat is found from coast to coast in North America, the roof rat is mainly relegated to the lower half of the east coast, the Gulf states and the west coast of the continent. Due to its extraordinary climbing talents, the roof rat makes easy work of trees, power and telephone lines, and even gutter spouts to facilitate its access to homes. The Norway rat can climb too, but tends to stay in the lower floors of multi-storey buildings, particularly when both species inhabit the same building. The Norway rat, weighing over four hundred grams, is 33 to 50 percent larger than the roof rat.

Being an excellent swimmer both above and under the water, the Norway rat has been known to pop in uninvited out of a toilet or basement drain. One was observed swimming twenty-four meters underwater, while another was able to swim non-stop for more than two and a half days.

Rats have poor eyesight and are colour-blind; they more than make up for this with their excellent powers of smell, touch, hearing and taste. For example, they can detect contaminants in their food as minute as 0.5 parts per million, a figure far below the human threshhold.

These two omnivorous species also differ somewhat in their food habits, though they are both gluttonous eaters. The roof rat with access to trees is quite content to gulp down fruits and nuts, as well as grains and vegetables. By contrast, the Norway rat prefers meat and, in fact, has a diet that would be considered nutritionally balanced for people. The Norway rat thrives on garbage and stored food. Both absolutely require water, between fifteen and thirty milliliters per day.

Neither species wanders very far; their home ranges are only about thirty to fifty meters in radius. But they're sure promiscuous; the rabbit's got nothing on these two characters. With spring and fall peaks for reproduction, both species begin breeding between two and three months of age. Females come into heat every four or five days, and they will mate again within a day or two of the birth of a litter. The gestation period is about twenty-two days. Both species have approximately four to seven litters per year, but the Norway rat has the edge by having between eight and twelve young per litter as opposed to only four to eight for the roof rat. Considering postnatal mortality though, both species wean about twenty young rats in the the world each year. One Norway rat and her young of the year produced another fifteen hundred rats in one year.

The life span of either species is one year. In an urban environment, a Norway rat has less than a 5 percent chance of surviving annually. It's well known that predators, pathogens and parasites are not important controls of their populations, so what does keep them in check? Well, next to humans, the Norway rat's biggest enemy is another Norway rat. Rats have a social organization; the larger ones and females with young are dominant. Hence, most rats fall prey to cannibalism.

Norway rats can gnaw through cinder blocks, lead sheeting and pipes, and aluminum siding. They can also climb inside vertical pipes only 40 millimeters in diameter and can squeeze through an opening 14 millimeters wide.

That just about summarizes the kind of critter we're up against. I certainly won't make any pleas for leaving them alone, and here's why: besides biting one in every one hundred thousand human city dwellers, including children, and contaminating our food and water with their hair, feces and urine, rats can transmit the plague (only the roof rat), murine typhus, trichinosis, salmonellosis, leptospirosis, and Rickettsial pox, to name but a few. Fortunately, they apparently do not transmit rabies. It's often been said that rat-borne diseases have taken more human lives than all the wars and revolutions in history. As for economics, one rat eats up to eighteen kilograms of food per year, but contaminates ten times that much with its droppings (over twenty-five thousand droppings per year). The damage to personal effects, buildings, electrical wires and lead pipes caused by their gnawing and burrowing can't be overlooked either.

Controlling the rat population is a problem. Essentially, we must remove their access to food, water, and shelter. The various signs indicating the presence of rats in your home are somewhat similar to those outlined for the house mouse. If you find old droppings and/or see one or more rats at night with a flashlight, you've got a problem. If you see fresh droppings and/or three or more at night or even one in the daytime, you've got a big problem.

Methods of rat control are beyond the scope of this book, and I urge you to contact your local pest-control people if you have a rat problem. In the meantime, keep all possible points of entry firmly sealed; they will enter existing holes but they won't necessarily make any. Keep them out of your neighbourhood by preventing dogs, cats and other wildlife from tearing open your garbage bags or tipping over your trash cans, as the odours and sight of food will attract them.

Two good things can be said about Norway rats. First, they eat house mice. More important though, we must remember that the white laboratory rat—an albino derivative of the Norway—has made enormous contributions to finding cures for disease, and solutions to innumerable biological problems.

BATS
a hit or a myth?

What do we know about bats? Well, they're a public menace because they get tangled in hair, bring bedbugs into the house, and spread rabies. Wrong, wrong, wrong! We could not have greater friend in nature's circle. Read on.

Of the nine hundred or so bat species in the world, about forty reside in North America. I won't bore you by listing all the different kinds, except to point out two basic types found in urban environments. Colonial bats include the little brown (probably the most abundant), the big brown, Mexican free-tailed, evening, pallid, and eastern pipistrelle. Red, hoary, and silver-haired bats comprise the solitary types, usually preferring to roost amid the leaves and under loose bark of shade trees near residential areas; they enter buildings only as transients.

Inclined to colonizing man-made structures, both the little and big brown bats are found coast to coast south of the tree line. The range of the evening bat, generally a tree dweller that also uses attics, is limited to the southeastern U.S. The red bat inhabits the southern parts of Canada and all of the U.S. except for the Rockies.

Some bats use night roosts for resting between feeding bouts or for socializing, but the main day-time roosts fall into one of four categories: 1) nursery roosts for the young; 2) summer male roosts where the segregated males hang out during nursing; 3) transient roosts during spring and fall (where most of the mating occurs); and 4) winter roosts. In mild climates, the winter roosts are simply resting places; in colder climates the bats actually hibernate there.

The little brown bat sets up its nurseries in attics, church belfries, and barn roofs; they particularly like hot, dark places with poor ventilation and several access holes. Little brown colonies can reach up to two thousand individuals. In contrast, the big brown bat prefers cooler, more ventilated locations and can thus be found in attics, out-buildings rafters, rock crevices, tree hollows, wall vines, under loose tarpaper, and even in cracks in concrete sports arenas. They number between twelve and two hundred in a single colony; forty-three were once found behind a house shutter, another favourite place. In winter, big browns hibernate in storm sewers and between the walls of heated buildings. Free-tailed bats in the southeastern states form both summer and winter roosts in buildings. One church belfry was known to house a colony of five hundred evening bats. Sometimes building roosts are shared by several species. As said above, solitary bats seldom enter buildings except as transients, but they're not averse to using the outside portions. Red bats often hang upside down in more exposed situations, looking very much like leaves. One woman found a silver-haired bat clinging to the folds of her shower curtain.

Most species show amazing abilities to home in on their roosts. One little brown bat that was released over four hundred kilometers away found its way home. In another study, bats released thirty-two kilometers away returned home the same night, those released sixty-four kilometers away by the second night, those ninety-six kilometers away by the third night, and those taken four hundred kilometers away by the fourth and fifth nights. Apparently adults home better than sub-adults. Blindfolded bats released eight kilometers away from their roosts returned home as quickly as sighted individuals, but most experts agree that though echo-location is important in short-distance homing, vision is critical over longer distances. Of course bats can see—they've got eyeballs, don't they? There's some controversy as to just how well they do see, but bats can definitely distinguish between light and dark and can detect large objects and physiographic features.

The most remarkable feature of bats, though, is their ability to echo-locate with sonar. Essentially, they emit ultrasonic sounds at roughly ten per second. During sudden manoeuvres, the frequency is increased up to two hundred per second. A minute muscle in the bat's ear contracts to prevent the bat from hearing its own cry, which would interfere with the incoming echo. With this feature they can perceive targets and background objects a hundred meters away. For an object fifteen centimeters from the bat's mouth, the time delay is one-thousandth of a second. Typically, the whole process of detection, pursuit and capture takes about one second.

As would be expected, bats keep those ear passages fastidiously clean by twisting the "thumb" of the forefoot in the ear during roosting. They also have well-developed scent glands in the form of swellings on the upper lip. Although olfaction plays a very minor role in food detection, musk is often emitted during excitement; suggested reasons for this are the attraction of mates, the location of roosting spots and maybe nursing young, and repelling enemies.

Bats do utter sounds audible to humans. If you're foolish enough to reach out to touch a bat with an unprotected hand, the sound to heed is a constant, irritated buzzing noise. Should you ignore this warning, you may be bitten.

Apparently voice signatures are used for identification by young bats and their mothers in the nursing colonies. The big brown bat can be recognized by its audible chatter during flight.

The little brown bat continually beats its wings at about fifteen strokes per second during flight, occasionally making short soaring sweeps. The average speed for most city-dwelling bats is between 10 and 25 kilometers per hour, but the big brown bat and the red bat have been clocked, over short distances, at 39 and 64 kilometers per hour, respectively. The weak, erratic flight of the eastern pipistrelle resembles that of a large moth or butterfly. Their lightness (approximately five grams for the pipistrelle and twenty grams for the big brown bat) facilitates their impressive flight capabilities.

If, by some rare miscalculation, a bat ends up in the drink, it can swim about sixty meters before exhaustion sets in. Providing the fur is not too wet, a lift-off from water can be made. Their crawling and climbing abilities are well-known to people with colonies in their attics.

Three of the bat species found in the southwest relish pollen, nectar and fruit, thus providing a valuable fertilizing service for plants and hence, humans. Insects, however, are the sole item on most North American bat menus. They are scooped up by the mouth, the cupped membrane of the tail, or the wing skin. Insectivorous bats have special jaw and tooth adaptations for capturing and eating both hard and soft insects. For example, the little brown bat eats flies, mosquitoes, moths, midges, caddisfies, and some beetles, whereas the big brown bat prefers mainly May and click beetles, flying ants, and houseflies. (Some persevering researcher spent countless hours analyzing over two thousand bat droppings to determine their diet.) The red bat is especially attracted to street lights and will even alight upon them to nab a tasty bug.

Bats can easily compete with even the fanciest electronic bug zapper. Consuming half its weight in insects per night, the litle brown munches seven or eight insects per minute, or about a hundred and forty in twenty minutes. Over a four-month period, a colony of one hundred bats takes in just over nineteen kilograms of insects. It has been estimated that a colony of five hundred bats can account for over five hundred thousand flying insects nightly; that's a lot of bugs.

The eastern pipistrelle bat is among the first to appear during the day, in late afternoon or on overcast days, and is usually the last to head for the roost after sunrise. The big brown bat has been observed flying in midday. Generally, though, most bats leave their roosts to feed at twilight. They'll eat for an hour or two and then rest.

YOU KNOW IT'S A MYTH, AND I KNOW IT'S A MYTH, BUT I JUST CAN'T RESIST THAT, CAN YOU?

Occasionally, bats will dip down to lap up some water. Oddly, some silver-haired bats have been caught in mousetraps baited with cheese and raisins; their young have fed on fly larvae in tree cavities. A captive big brown once ate some of his smaller inmates. Bats have also been maintained on a diet of mealworms.

Because of extreme but predictable variations in their insect food supply, migration and hibernation are necessities for bats. Although big brown bats and red bats can tolerate freezing temperatures, virtually all bats hibernate by accumulating body fat before entering into a state of torpor in a winter roost with a stable, cool environment. Deep hibernation can last two or three months. Their heartbeat, normally six hundred beats per minute, drops to between ten and eighty beats, while their body temperature assumes that of the roost wall. The big brown bat inhales about twenty-five to fifty times per minute for roughly three minutes and then actually stops breathing for up to eight minutes. In as little as seven minutes, a bat can rouse itself from this state into full flight. Occasionally some species do leave their shelters even on extremely cold days either to avoid temperature fluctuations or to satisfy mid-winter mating urges.

All North American bats are promiscuous. Reproduction takes place in autumn, winter and early spring for most species. Mating generally occurs in the roosts, but red bats have been observed attempting to copulate on the wing. The sperm can be stored within the males or in the female's uterus until ovulation and fertilization occur in the spring. The young are born between April and July. For example, in Vermont, nursing colonies of twelve to twelve hundred individuals are established in attics as early as April 22. Gestation takes place over fifty to sixty days for the little brown, and between seventy-five and ninety days for the red and free-tailed bats. The litter usually consists of one, rarely two young; the red bat, however, has three to four young at a time.

The naked newborn of the little brown bat weighs 1.5 grams, about one-quarter to one-fifth of their mother's size. Closed at birth, its eyes will open the next day. In most species, the female nurses only her own young, therefore vocal signatures and olfactory cues are important for identification in large colonies. In contrast, female free-tails suckle anyone's young. Clinging with a vice-like grip on their mother's teats, the sucklings have been known to take a ride with her during a change in roosts. One red bat was seen carrying three or four babies whose combined weight exceeded her own.

Young bats can fly at three or four weeks, are weaned at six weeks, and are full-grown at about two months of age.

Nursery colonies disperse after weaning in July and August. Most North American female bats can breed in their first year, but males often wait until the second summer. The reproductive rate is high; 90 to 98 percent breed each season.

Bats are capable of living to ripe old ages. Little brown bats have made it to thirty years of age, while big brown bats as old as nineteen have been recorded. When one considers the high mortality among young bats and an approximated 25 percent decline among adult females annually, most bats are lucky to see their tenth birthday. One estimate of the average life span of the female little brown bat is between 1.2 and 2.2 years.

While the proliferation of buildings over the last century has multiplied the numbers of little and big brown bats, their increased use of buildings must be, in part, a response to the loss of natural roosts. Indeed, many bat populations have suffered dramatic declines across North America. For example, numbers of the little brown bat in Indiana and northern Kentucky have dropped from sixteen thousand to just over three thousand in one decade.

A major cause for these declines must be the extermination or exclusion of nursing colonies in buildings. In one place, 52 percent of twenty-three colonies of little brown bats were lost in ten years. Chemical pesticides such as DDT not only kill off much of the bats' insect food, but they also poison the bats indirectly via the food chain. Disturbances to winter roosts by vandals, cave explorers, and irresponsible researchers and banders result in depleted fat reserves, which spells death for many wintering bats. Bats have their problems with Mother Nature, too. Many young die after entering winter roosts without enough body fat. Young nursing bats that fall from the roost are not recovered. Various accidents, such as collisions with cars, buildings, barbed wire fences, and even burdock burrs, do occur, despite their "radar." Storms during migration kill a good number. Finally, hawks, owls, red-winged blackbirds, grackles, blue jays, rat snakes, leopard frogs, black bass, and the usual assortment of four-legged predators take their toll as well.

Many homeowners play landlord to single bats or colonies without even realizing it. Outside your home, bats will hide themselves either under or behind shutters, wood shingles, roofing, drain gutters, awnings, overhang trim, chimney flashing, tarpaper, or inside garages, patios, porches, outbuildings, root cellars, wells, sewers and, yes, even graveyard crypts. Church belfries are entered via unscreened louvers. Bats can enter homes through open windows, unscreened fireplaces, and just about any tiny, narrow slit, crack or crevice in a building. The small species

IS ··· ER ··· SOMEONE THERE ??

can squeeze through a hole smaller than the size of a dime. Specifically, the little brown bat needs a hole 1.6 by 2.2 centimeters, whereas the big brown requires one 3.2 by 1.3 centimeters. Favourite entry places of the big brown bat include the roof overhang or eaves, crevices between the outer wall and chimney, cracks around windows, and holes caused by loose or ill-fitting boards or bricks. Once inside, they literally hang about—in attics, cornices, fascias, walls, between roofs and ceilings, as well as windows and screens, chimneys, around drainpipes, and occasionally in crawlspaces. (Are you still sure you've never played landlord to a bat or two?)

If you hear squeaking, scratching, scrambling and crawling in the attic, don't jump to conclusions; chimney swifts, as well as mice, rats, and squirrels also invade upper parts of houses. Odours may be a giveaway, but fecal droppings and stains near eaves, beneath entrance holes, and below roosts are a good indication of the presence of bats. Unlike other mammal's feces, bat droppings can easily be crushed between the fingers, contain shiny bits of undigested insects, but are not comprised of that white, chalky material. Bat guano does attract roaches and mites, and the odour is pungent. Sometimes the weight of bat guano can cause a ceiling to sag or even cave in. (One house had over five hundred liters of guano removed from it!) Some researchers have reported "stalactites" of crystallized urine hanging from building rafters. On the bright side though, guano does make terrific fertilizer. If you wish to remove it, wet it down first and wear a respirator to avoid potentially fatal histoplasmosis, a fungal disease caught from airborne spores.

Speaking of disease, what's the truth about bats and rabies? OK, rabies has been reported in thirty of the forty species in all parts of North America, but during the last forty years, only ten people have died in the U.S.A. from contracting rabies from bats (two of these were airborne-derived in caves containing enormous numbers of bats; this is not a health hazard in houses). More people die of dog bites, bee stings or even from direct lightning strikes each year than from bats.

The best advice is simply to refrain from handling them without gloves, forceps or a stick. Anti-rabies vaccinations will save your pets from being destroyed, too. If you are bitten, wash the bite thoroughly with soap and water and seek medical help immediately. Bringing in the offending bat for examination may also save you from painful rabies treatments.

And what about those nasty bedbugs? Essentially, this is just another myth. They do carry bedbugs, but they're not the same variety that infests humans. Bats also carry the usual ticks, mites and fleas, which rarely bite people.

If a single bat accidentally enters your home, the best reaction is not to scream and run around in a panic. Instead, open all the doors and windows that lead outside (close all the others) and turn off all the lights to prevent it from merely hiding. The fresh air currents will help it find its way out. Otherwise, it can be caught in a net, small box or can, or by a gloved hand or a towel thrown over it. If you can't handle any of these methods, call for professional help.

Healthy bats tend to avoid humans. If one does land on you, it's only because it's disoriented. That bats purposefully entangle themselves in hair is also a myth.

Temporary roosts do no harm and should be left alone unless the droppings become a problem. If a nursing colony grows too large and creates unwanted conflicts, the bats must go. Sadly, eviction has been tried with tear gas, sulphur candles, auto exhaust, cyanide, and DDT. These methods are useless either because they are painfully slow or because they're ineffective in killing all of the bats, thereby scattering sick bats all over the place, perhaps near children or pets. Some of these methods also constitute a human health hazard, but most importantly, they're all temporary. The last point also goes for the following inexpensive "remedies" that may or may not work: moth-repellent chemicals (see the chapter on skunks), high-frequency dog whistles blown by aquarium pumps, floodlighting the attic, coating the roost with grease or some other sticky stuff (all of which lose their tackiness with dust anyway), and creating drafts with an electric fan.

The best way to deal with unwanted bats is *exclusion*. (Besides, if you plug up any holes, you'll save on energy costs.) Simple homemade devices of tissue, light plastic or lighted candles can detect air currents. More elaborate (and expensive) devices for the same purpose can be bought. Once found, the entrance holes should be sealed in the fall after the young have left and after dark while the bats are feeding. Bat counts before sealing up the last opening will ensure that none are trapped inside. Again, special devices with one-way doors are now commercially available. Plugging can be achieved by caulking, flashing, screening, and insulation. Weatherstripping, stainless steel wool, and rustproof scouring pads will block long narrow cracks. Fiberglass or rockwool can be blown into wall spaces when the bats are absent. Finally, church steeples can be purged of bat problems by installing fiberglass over the inside tarpaper or .63 cm wire mesh over the inside of louvers.

Personally, as a homeowner in mosquito country, I don't mind sharing my place with a modest number of these harmless and beneficial creatures.

BIRDS
too few and too many

No other class of animal better illustrates our polarized views towards sharing our habitats with wildlife than do birds. Mention the names cardinal, bluejay or robin to suburban homeowners and you'll find that over 90 percent of them are glad to have these birds around. However, drop the names house sparrow, starling and pigeon into the conversation, and the figure drops to about 50 percent or lower.

Pigeons

The two extreme views are best shown by the case of the pigeon. If you stroll through any major city core, you'll surely encounter some kind soul dumping bags of bread crumbs among a horde of hungry pigeons. The mere suggestion that pigeon numbers are in need of control is enough to rouse some of these gentle people to physical violence.

You'll find pigeons in virtually every city and large town in North America, and that includes Hawaii. Nearly everyone can recognize them. (Well, there was one gentleman who had me drive into Montreal at breakneck speed to rescue a pigeon that he thought was a falcon.)

Where did they all come from? Pigeons are descended from the European rock dove, which was introduced to North America as a domesticated bird. The inevitable escapees proliferated in both rural and urban environments because they thrive on grain, seeds, garbage, and even insects if the other foods are scarce.

A pair takes eighteen days to incubate a clutch of one or two eggs, and the young leave the nest between four and six weeks of age. Before they even leave though, the female has laid another set of eggs. Pigeons breed virtually year-round, especially in the spring and fall. They're capable of living for three or four years in the wild and up to fifteen years in captivity.

With their highly varied plumage and their impressive aerial skills, many people find them attractive. Feeding them in city centers has even become a recreational activity for some people. In contrast, there are others who would wish every pigeon off the face of the earth, usually building owners who find the pigeons' messy nests and droppings at odds with the aesthetics and maintenance of their structures.

LONG LIVE THE UPPER CLASS!!

Often the argument of a human health threat is thrown at pigeon lovers. Is there really a danger of disease transmission from some birds to people in urban areas? The answer is yes. Far from being harmless, pigeons have the potential for transmitting over thirty diseases to humans. Most of these result from microscopic organisms living in pigeon feces or ectoparasites hiding among the feathers.

Histoplasmosis, probably the most common disease spread by pigeons and other wildlife in concentrated numbers (see the chapter on bats), results from inhaling the spores of the fungus *Histoplasma capsulatum* along with dust particles spread by the wind. Just a few spores are enough to cause a mild case, and in some areas 95 percent of the human population may be infected. Often misdiagnosed as flu, some people aren't aware they've been infected, while others may acquire immunity without realizing it. Histoplasmosis can become chronic though. Other fungal diseases transmitted in this manner include aspergillosus, candidiasis and cryptococcosis.

Another potentially dangerous disease that is airborne in dust from pigeon feces is ornithosis. This disease comes from a virus-like agent carried by a number of birds, but causing no symptoms in them. Ninety-nine percent of all cases, which resemble pneumonia, are mild. Encephali-

tis, meningitis and Newcastle's disease are other viral diseases transmitted by pigeons.

Salmonellosis, more than a form of food poisoning, can also be spread by pigeons; bacteria are left wherever the birds defecate. Trampling over their feces on window ledges and air intake vents, the pigeons stir up the bacteria in the dust that enters buildings via air conditioners and ventilators. Other bacterial diseases carried by pigeons include listeriosis, pasteurellosis, and yersiniosis.

We mustn't leave out the protozoan diseases such as American trypanosomiasis, trichomoniasis, and toxoplasmosis, perhaps one of the most widespread animal-transmitted diseases in North America. Lastly, you can also contract chlamydiosis, Q fever, and a number of diseases involving parasitic worms from pigeons. Detailed descriptions of these illnesses are beyond the scope of this book; you can almost certainly get details from your family doctor.

If all of the above sounds like a rallying call for the extermination of the pigeon in urban and suburban centers, you're wrong. I only want you to be aware of the potential dangers of attracting pigeons to your windowsills and balconies, as well as make pigeon lovers think a bit before coming out against some humane way of keeping pigeon numbers down to an enjoyable level.

DID YOU READ THIS NONSENSE ABOUT CHROMOSOME DAMAGE AND INSECTICIDES??

Besides not feeding them, there are ways of discouraging them from nesting and roosting on your property, but none of them is quick and cheap. As far as I know, the so-called frightening devices such as hawk or owl decoys, revolving lights, rubber snakes, reflective or brightly coloured strips of plastic, and ultrasonic sound do not work. Essentially, scare techniques like loud noises or streams of water must be used persistently to drive pigeons away for good. In real tight spaces, naphthalene flakes spread quite liberally around might work, but the odour could be strong enough to drive out the human occupants as well.

If you've got a pigeon problem, the only effective way to discourage them is to alter their roosting surface. Installing metal or wooden floors on ledges at a 45° angle, or laying down commercially available metal prongs will discourage pigeons. They have been known to construct their nests right on the prongs, though. Blocking up any entry points with appropriate construction materials and screening ornamental architecture with 2.54 cm wire mesh may be necessary. Some buildings have resorted to expensive electric wire systems that repel pigeons by shocking, but not killing them. For apartment dwellers with pigeons on their balconies, I recommend the temporary hanging of some inexpensive netting over the balcony until the pigeons establish themselves elsewhere.

Sparrows

The pigeon is not the most numerous bird in the city. That honour is bestowed upon the tiny house sparrow. Mostly described as brown and chunky, the males can be recognized by their black bibs and white cheek patches.

Its diet is even more varied than the pigeon's. Grain, fruit, seeds, and garden plants comprise 96 percent of the menu, but house sparrows are not averse to munching on bread crumbs and refuse from fast-food outlets.

Almost as prolific as rats, they breed year-round (mostly March to August) and produce between three and seven eggs per clutch. The eggs hatch after about ten or fourteen days of incubation, and the young leave the nest about two weeks later. They'll live up to five years in the wild; one zoo specimen made it to twenty-three.

What harm can these tiny creatures do? With their sheer numbers, they annoy gardeners by pecking at seeds, seedlings, buds, flowers, and maturing fruits and vegetables. They also can disseminate a good number of the diseases attributed to pigeons, and the chattering of their sometimes huge flocks can constitute a nuisance. House sparrows also gang up on more beneficial birds such as bluebirds and purple martins, destroying their eggs and young, and taking over their nests.

I DON'T <u>CARE</u> IF IT'S HARMLESS,··· JUST CLOSE THE DRAPES!!

Sound repellents don't work at all, and visual repellents like scarecrows or shiny foil strips are of limited effectiveness. If sparrows are entering your home, you can exclude them by covering any openings larger than 2 centimeters with solid material or poultry mesh. The 45°-angle ledge suggested for pigeons also works with sparrows. Ivy-covered walls, a favourite habitat, can be covered with plastic bird netting, which is available at most large plant nurseries. The same goes for small gardens. Drilling a 3 centimeter hole in the roof of bluebird houses and covering it with mesh will make them undesirable to sparrows; apparently the bluebirds don't mind a little rain. If sparrows are gobbling up all the feed on your feeder, you might try throwing some inexpensive bird food, such as bread crumbs, on the ground away from the feeder to draw them away.

Starlings

There's one more little rascal that has pitted itself against urban residents on many occasions. From less than two hundred individuals released in 1890 and 1891 by a man who wanted New York's Central Park to contain all the species mentioned in Shakespeare's plays, the starling now numbers more than 140 million in the U.S.A. alone.

Robin-sized and dark with light speckles, the starling nests in holes and cavities in trees, birdhouses, buildings and rocks. Four to seven eggs are laid and incubated for between eleven and thirteen days. After three weeks, the young fledge; two broods are raised each season.

Also versatile in its feeding habits, the starling will eat fruit, seeds (both wild and cultivated types), insects and other invertebrates, and of course, garbage. Flocks comprised of hundreds of thousands of birds will roost within towns; they will fly up to fifty kilometers to feeding sites.

As for building entry, all openings larger than 2.54 centimeters should be sealed off. The suggestions made earlier for sparrows and pigeons can also be applied to starlings. For bird-lovers, the starling's most obnoxious habit is its competition for nest sites with more desirable hole-nesters like bluebirds, flickers, purple martins, and American kestrels. Providing nest boxes with bright interiors will discourage starlings.

Woodpeckers

It's hard to dislike the industrious woodpeckers, but as long as we use wood as a building material and as long as we prize ornamental and fruit trees, not everyone will be a fan of theirs. The hairy, downy, and red-headed woodpeckers, as well as the yellow-bellied sapsucker and the common flicker, are the most abundant in North America, and the ones most likely encountered in

YOU KNOW, EVOLUTION IS REALLY QUITE FRIGHTENING.

suburbia. They share some characteristics. Short legs with two of the four toes pointing backwards—each with sharp claws—and stiff tail feathers help to keep the woodpecker on tree trunks. Drilling is done with a stout, pointed beak; a long, mobile tongue dislodges larvae or ants from the wood or bark. Some woodpecker tongues have strong teeth and spikes pointing backwards like barbs for spearing insects. Large salivary glands lubricate the tongue to make it sticky.

Most woodpeckers feed on tree-living or wood-boring insects, but a few like the flicker feed on ground insects such as ants. Still others feed on mature berries, fruit, nuts and certain seeds, while the sapsucker specializes in tree sap, cambium, phloem (the inner layers of bark), and insects.

Even where trees are scarce, you'll find woodpeckers boring into wooden fence posts, utility poles, and buildings, and it's not always for the purpose of food, either. Sapsuckers drill into sound, insect-free wood to obtain sap, while acorn woodpeckers will chisel out acorn-sized holes to store—you guessed it—acorns. In the spring, though, any old woodpecker may be heard hammering away on not just a wooden surface, but on metal objects like gutters, drainpipes, chimney caps, television antennas, and so on. This drumming activity serves to establish territories and to attract or signal potential mates. Sometimes repeated

as frequently as six hundred times daily, it can be just a tad annoying to human ears.

The biggest complaint against woodpeckers comes from those with wooden homes in suburbia. Holes in wooden siding, eaves or sideboards, especially cedar or redwood, can be attributed to as many as eight birds in a season. Of course, the woodpeckers are not just tearing your siding to pieces for fun. They are likely after insect larvae hiding out in various grooves or gaps in the siding. By getting rid of the insects, you may also solve your woodpecker problem.

Just as you probably do, woodpeckers—particularly sapsuckers—have a few favourite trees in your backyard. Repeated attacks on fruit or nut trees result in enlarged holes and the loss of a fair amount of bark. Girdling (completely removing the bark in a band around the tree) the trunk or even a limb can kill the tree, as the wounds invite injurious insects, diseases, or wood-decaying organisms.

To discourage woodpeckers from damaging your homes or backyard trees, it is imperative you take action before they establish their territory and hence become more persistent. Loud noises or constant harassment might work at first, but the only long-term solution is exclusion. Lightweight nylon or plastic netting can be draped or secured

O.K!! O.K!! I'LL PUT OUT SOME DAMN SUET!!

over the pecked areas, but should be at least 7.6 centimeters out from the surface to be effective. Metal barriers such as aluminum flashing will work; however, if given a foothold, woodpeckers can actually drill through it. If you have a choice in the first place, a house constructed of aluminum siding, harder compressed wood, or wood-fiber siding will prevent any future problems.

On damaged trees, barriers of hardware cloth, plastic or loosely wrapped burlap should halt further destruction. Taste and odour repellents do not work. Neither are plastic twirlers, windmills, reflective strips, and hawk, owl or snake replicas very effective, let alone aesthetic. Sticky or tacky repellents that may work on valuable trees are commercially available, but they may discolour house siding.

The nicest solution, which works more often than not, is to attract the little devils away from your home and trees by supplying them with ample quantities of suet. In summer it will be necessary to reheat the suet once or twice to make it hard-packed. It should also be kept in the shade or it will become rancid and may cause baldness in woodpeckers, and there's hardly a sadder sight than a bald bird.

Swallows

Even the beautiful and highly beneficial cliff swallow incurs the wrath of suburban homeowners. Found throughout most of North America, and the only square-tailed species, the cliff swallow can be recognized by its pale orange-brown rump, white forehead, rust-coloured throat, and steel-blue crown and back. It has four requirements for survival: open habitats in which to catch insects, a body of fresh water, a vertical surface beneath an overhang or ledge for nesting, and a handy supply of mud to construct the nest with.

Food comes in the form of bees, wasps, ants, beetles, flies, and other flying bugs; the swallows will fly as far away as 6.4 kilometers to find them. Nest locations in the suburbs are readily available on buildings, bridges, and overpasses. Their nests are generally gourd-shaped, enclosed mud structures lined inside with grass, hair and feathers. A single nest might be composed of up to fifteen hundred mud pellets, each representing one trip, sometimes up to almost a kilometer away. Splashes of fecal matter on the wall around the nest will announce the arrival of newly hatched young; therein lies the trouble for some building owners. Occasionally the mud nests fall to the ground as well. Worse, some of the nests are appropriated by sparrows, and they're much less pleasant guests.

YOU WANT <u>HOW</u> MUCH FOR PROTECTION??

It's illegal to remove a swallow's nest without a government permit (as is the case for all protected birds in Canada and the U.S.A.), so if you don't wish to host these rather innocuous birds, the best solution is exclusion. Before they arrive in the spring, cover the nesting area with 1.3 to 2.5 cm plastic net or poultry wire, either stretched taut or hanging straight down. Panels of fiberglass, glass, or sheetmetal installed under the overhang will make it difficult for the swallows to attach their nests.

If it's not such a big problem, you might just wait them out. Often, for reasons still not understood, the colonies are abandoned after two or three years of use. In the meantime, take solace in the bug control, free of charge.

Crows

Widely distributed across North America and one of the best-known birds, the clever crow is a common sight in suburbia. These omnivorous critters have over six hundred items on their menu. Consuming between eight and ten meals per day, a crow's daily intake equals about a quarter-pounder's worth. Their eating habits are not among the favourite of bird lovers, as crows are not shy about robbing nests for eggs and young.

Their lifespan in the wild is usually between five and ten years, depending on how much trouble they get into. The crow's reputation for intelligence is well earned, too. They can count up to four, solve puzzles, and even mimic sounds—including human ones like "mama," "papa," "hello," and "howdy-do." But not everybody appreciates their vocal talents, especially at four or five in the morning. If the noise is quite regular, chances are that they're nesting nearby in an oak, pine, cottonwood or elm tree. The four to six eggs take eighteen days to hatch, and fortunately for some homeowners, crows only raise one brood a year. You might be thankful your home is not located near a major roost, which might house several million crows at a time.

There's precious little that can be done about the noise from a nest, but it's only for a short breeding season and not year-round. In some cases, a flock of crows might have stumbled upon a roosting owl, which they love to torment and the disturbance will be very temporary. Unfortunately, the only means of discouraging their presence is somewhat dramatic, that is chopping down all potential nest trees within earshot; maybe earplugs would be more appropriate.

Gulls

In many towns and cities, herring and ring-billed gulls are attracted to landfill sites and quarries. Some populations have developed interesting feeding patterns that coincide with the morning openings of fast-food outlets. On a rainy day, you can often see them sitting about an expansive grassy surface, like an athletic field; they're feeding on worms flooded from their burrows. The only real complaint about gulls is their sometimes excessive squawking. Until landfill sites are made less attractive to them, this problem will remain with us.

Attracting Birds

Thus far we've addressed only those species that have conflicted with the interests of city dwellers. There is another side to the coin: birds add colour, music and life to our sometimes monotonous and desolate cityscapes. Bird appreciation is second only to gardening as North America's favourite pastime. Let's face it—birds have wings and they can go anywhere. For example, within the Beltway, a highway circling downtown Washington, D.C., you can see at one time or another one-quarter of all bird species that visit or reside in North America.

Mallard ducks cavort in ponds, lakes and man-made reservoirs in city centres. Nighthawks, as their name implies, swoop after insects on summer nights and raise their young on flat, gravelled roofs. Pheasants and sometimes ruffed grouse wander through city parks, occasionally entering a wooded backyard. Screech owls frequent tangled vines in suburban areas, while their larger cousin, the great horned owl, hides and hunts among wooded ravines. American kestrels and merlins are two small falcon species that have adapted to nesting in our cities. Even the world's fastest diving bird, the peregrine falcon, feeds its young high atop the ledges of the tallest skyscrapers. And who hasn't seen a robin hopping across a well-groomed lawn in search of that early worm, or for that matter, a brilliant red cardinal foraging among the hardwoods?

Birds have four basic needs: food, water, protective cover, and a place to breed. There's much that urban or suburban residents can do to enhance their neighbourhoods for these feathered critters. You can start by altering the habitat in your own backyard.

Some of the most popular tall trees among birds are crab-apple, walnut, tupelo, mulberry, sweetgum and sassafras. These are not enough, though. Clusters of shade-loving small trees and shrubs like sumac, cherry, dogwood, serviceberry, holly, privet, viburnum and witchhazel planted under the tall ones for some ground cover are absolutely ideal. If you're in a hurry, planting a cluster of fast-growing species like oak, honey locust or red maple,

YOU WANT ME TO SIGN A PETITION TO KEEP THE TOWN DUMP <u>OPEN</u>??

or some small fruiting shrubs like honeysuckle or cultivated berry bushes will make your yard a favourite restaurant for birds.

If your yard is big enough, try leaving some treed areas in open soil or mulched with leaf litter. Open expanses of lawn broken up by clusters of flowers or shrubs will provide flyways for visiting birds. Since some species enjoy nesting, feeding or roosting in evergreens, a balance of conifers and hardwoods is especially attractive. The same can be said for dead trees, as long as there is no danger of them falling over. Cut them off at about three or four meters, leaving a few branches up to a meter long.

Dense shrubs and hedges like firethorn, boxwood, holly, privet or yew planted along walkways, patios or yard edges, and left largely unclipped, provide excellent food sources and cover for many songbirds. Vines such as honeysuckle, ivy or creepers planted along the foundations of your home provide ideal cover for small birds.

A number of flower species can provide a winter seed supply for many birds. These include such perennials as asters, columbine and goldenrod, as well as annual flowers like cosmos, zinnias, marigolds, and probably the favourite of all, sunflowers. Several grass species, such as quaking grass and love grass, are also excellent food sources. If you only have a little room, planter boxes of flowers and deciduous or evergreen shrubs, such as boxwood, yew, juniper and holly, will fill the bill. Even windowsills with flowerboxes will attract birds.

Obviously, some people might desire the birds' presence, but harbour mixed feelings towards them if they conflict with their number-one pastime—gardening. Frankly, hanging out shiny fluttering objects or snake or hawk decoys are only temporary and often ineffective deterrents to marauding birds. The only realistic long-term solution is exclusion. Most garden centres sell bird netting that can be placed directly over your fruit trees or on a frame over gardens or seed beds. Cheesecloth sacks over grape and corn plants work well, but may entail a lot of effort. Strings hung tautly over and through valuable plants apparently make alighting uncomfortable for many bird species.

Several surveys in large towns have shown that just over 40 percent of all residents have birdfeeders out for some portion of the year. If you're going to feed birds, you should do so consistently, particularly in the cold months. Some birds do come to rely on the handouts. If you must leave the feeder for a time, then a gradual reduction in the food supply will give the birds the message. Actually, so many people are feeding them now that the birds probably make the rounds of the neighbourhood anyway.

LET ME GET THIS STRAIGHT, DEAR. WE'RE NOT
GOING SOUTH BECAUSE THEY DIDN'T GO SOUTH?

If you don't want to be responsible for dead birds, another rule is to avoid leaving out moldy, spoiled food. Baked goods (which birds eat readily) are prone to becoming moldy very quickly. Although many fine commercial mixes are available, you can save money by buying seed in bulk and storing it in rodent-proof garbage cans. Among the best seeds are sunflower, millet (especially white millet), and thistleseed. Nutmeats, table scraps (that aren't too spicy), and canned dog food are all eaten by birds. If you've got lots of money, pecans and walnuts are a real treat. Some people secure halves of fresh fruit or coconuts to a feeder or a branch for the orioles and tanagers.

Suet, of course, is a favourite among many backyard feeding operations. Beef or mutton suet (not the stringy kind) melted down and then mixed with seeds or fruits is ideal. As said earlier, leaving it out in weather above 23° C may make it go rancid.

Some people put out peanut butter for its high protein content and attractiveness to many birds. At least one experienced feeder warns against its use, though; apparently it will stick to the roof of the mouth of the tiny chickadee, causing it to choke to death.

You can do the seed-eating birds like finches and grosbeaks a big favour by supplying them with some grit like coarse sand or crushed oyster shell during the winter months. It will be used to grind up the hard seeds in the bird's gizzard.

Feeding birds can consist of simply throwing the food onto a cleared area on the ground, but there are many feeders on the market. Basically, your feeder should protect the food from extreme weather conditions and dispense the food as needed. Some birds like the feeders placed high up, while others prefer feeding at ground level. It should not be placed too close to your house, but certainly in a place where it is visible so you can enjoy it. Nearby cover or perches for predators like hawks should be eliminated, and guards to prevent squirrels getting at it can be installed (see the chapter on squirrels). If your feeder is inundated with undesirable feathered free-loaders like sparrows, starlings or pigeons, you might offer them some less expensive food on the ground away from the feeder.

Hummingbirds

Hummingbirds are among the most delightful of backyard guests. Three species—Anna's, ruby-throated, and rufous—are the most popular. Weighing just over three grams, their wings beat an almost incredible seventy-five times per second. For migrations, which may cover over three thousand kilometers, a hummingbird may increase its bodyweight by fifty percent.

If you're planting flowers for them, bright red, orange or pink tubular flowers are best. Artificial feeders containing a sugar solution of one part white sugar to four parts water are very effective. Mould should be avoided by not using honey and by cleaning out the bottle every week.

You mustn't underestimate the importance of water to birds year-round. Fresh, clean, uncontaminated water offered in plastic tubs or dishes, hollowed out logs, holes lined with plastic, or even a mist spray (hummingbirds like this) is highly attractive to them. A rough surface for proper footing, a gradual shallow approach, and a depth between three and seven centimeters is absolutely ideal. Concrete or cement baths are more practical than wooden or metal ones. If the water is audible, that is if there is a waterfall or dripping hose, the birds will be attracted all the more quickly.

Birds don't just visit suburban or urban areas to feed. Many species commonly raise their young in this habitat, and you can have them nesting right in your backyard. Given their territorial natures and unless the species is colonial, as are swallows, for example, you'll likely only attract one pair of a particular species.

Nesting materials like yarn, string, narrow strips of soft cloth, absorbent cotton, pet fur, feathers and excelsior in pieces less than twenty centimeters long can be offered in wire baskets. Swallows and robins appreciate a ready supply of wet, sticky clay.

Birdhouses

With our inclination to rid ourselves of old, decaying trees, it's no wonder that over fifty species of birds readily use birdhouses. Simple houses made of durable, weather-resistant wood like redwood or white cedar, and stained either brown, gray or green are best. This type of building material, well-insulated from the cold and heat, will breathe, but still keep the birds dry. Installed on a pole or branch with appropriate predator guards, the birdhouse should be securely fastened with its opening facing away from prevailing weather. Robins, phoebes and swallows will happily use nesting shelves placed under your house eaves. An annual cleaning out of debris, followed by fumigation once the birds are gone for the winter, will keep the birds coming back.

If you want to play landlord to the ultimate in mosquito control, a purple martin house could be the answer. You might start with a structure containing between eight and twelve apartments on a pole between three-and-a-half and six meters above the ground. Martins will be most

IT'S A LEASE - BREAKING PARTY !!

attracted to a house on an open lawn some twelve meters away from any flight obstructions. Nearby telephone and utility wires for perching and a body of water for feeding will also make the site more attractive to them.

You can build martin homes from wood, but I heartily recommend the commercially made aluminum ones. They're light (and therefore easy to put up and take down) and weather resistant, with a life-time finish. They also have heat-reflective exteriors and plenty of ventilation. Their shiny interiors will discourage starlings, and plugs (removed only when the martins appear in the spring) will keep out the sparrows. A nice touch is a guard barrier around the walkways that prevents the young from falling before they can fly. Some martin landlords never clean out their houses, with no apparent detriment to their birds and their young, but most experts recommend fumigating with sulfur before and during the middle of the breeding season to control mites and fleas effectively. Sprinkle about one tablespoon round the edges of each nest, avoiding getting it on the eggs or young.

One last consideration for suburban homeowners is the birds who die from colliding with picture windows. Indeed, some birds will actually attack their own reflections in an effort to drive off a supposed intruder. Such behavior can be averted by keeping your drapes closed during the day or by hanging strips of material on the outside of the window. Apparently, silhouettes of hawks and falcons stuck on the window are effective to a certain degree.

More and more species will be forced to adapt to our cities over the next few decades. Some will become welcome friends, others will join the ranks of what we perceive as nuisance birds. It has been and always will be a love-hate relationship.

THE HERPTILES
the slithery, scaly, slimy, and slow

For the most part, reptiles and amphibians—collectively known as the herptiles—have gotten a raw deal from urbanization. The modification of their habitat by brush-burning, land-filling, and drainage schemes is a major factor in the decline in their populations and is sometimes the cause of their extinction. Besides causing direct mortalities, chemical pollution is responsible for the destruction of environmental components necessary to various life stages, as well as undesirable changes in behavior, morphology and resistance to disease. Our roads constitute barriers to their travel. In seeking warmth, some snakes and turtles gravitate towards roadsides, where they are ultimately crushed by vehicles. Compounding the above is the largely negative public attitude towards slithery, scaly or slimy creatures. Indeed, most snakes are killed on sight, at least by those not scared to death of them. Still other specimens like the box turtle are collected by greedy pet dealers, by children and teachers for school projects, and by others "just for fun."

In spite of all of the above, a small number of reptiles and amphibians are either holding their own or increasing their numbers within city boundaries. Increased food and cover, along with decreased numbers of natural predators, may be the cause. The construction of reservoirs in some cities and towns has benefited turtle and toad populations. Dense numbers of insects attracted to urban lighting lead to toad picnics, especially when there are no snakes around, one of the toads' chief predators. And no one really knows how many of those little pet shop turtles released into city ponds, creeks and reservoirs actually survive.

Snakes

Just the word *snake* is enough to cause heart palpitations in some people. Usually such overreactions are the result of some previous, unpleasant experience. Generally, snakes are not very mobile and remain largely inactive, hibernating in the winter months and sunbathing in the summer, with occasional hunting forays for insects, earthworms, small mammals, toads, frogs, and small birds. One decent meal can last a snake for several weeks. Although they haven't any ears whatsoever, or eyelids (except for a protective transparent cap), snakes can smell by using their long, forked tongues to lick gaseous particles from

the air and inserting them into the Jacobson's organ, a two-holed structure in the roof of the mouth. Loosely connected lower jaws, highly stretchable skin, and a special breathing tube to prevent choking, facilitate the swallowing of prey much larger than itself.

The non-poisonous milk, corn, bull and fox snakes can occasionally be encountered in suburban backyards. However, three species of snakes do quite well in urban centres. These include the eastern garter, the northern brown, and the red-bellied snakes. The eastern garter snake, probably the most common of all, ranges from 45 to 135 centimeters in length, but most are between 63 and 81 centimeters. There are probably enough variations in race and colour among the garter snakes to give a herpetologist a nervous breakdown. Generally, the base colour is greenish, black or brown, and the stripes are yellowish, orange, or reddish. There are even garter snakes that are all black with a white throat and chin.

Garter snakes feed primarily on earthworms, frogs, mice, slugs, snails, and leeches. Both live and dead foods are eaten. Occasionally, these snakes will even venture into water to capture minnows.

Unlike the egg-laying snakes, garter snakes give birth to live young in late summer or early fall, usually having between ten and thirty in a litter. (One snake produced a record eighty-seven young.) Contrary to popular opinion, snakes do not swallow their young to protect them; their strong digestive juices would probably kill their offspring.

Sometimes as many as ten thousand garter snakes will den together for the winter, and a number of people complain each spring about the sudden appearance of these creatures in their homes. They will bite if handled or cornered, but the wound will only consist of some small scratches resulting in mild swelling and redness. The garter snake's best defense is the release of a foul-smelling scent, originating from the tail end, that is smeared over anyone trying to handle it.

The northern brown snake, likely the most abundant serpent in New York City, can be recognized by its grayish-brown or beige colour, with a light stripe down the centre of the back and a row of small, dark flecks on either side, giving it a tweedy appearance. An average length for this snake is between 30 and 43 centimeters. Sadly, this harmless and gentle creature, which never bites, is sometimes mistaken for a baby massasauga rattler. Requiring some dampness in its environment, the inconspicuous brown snake prefers to hide under boards, logs, and flat stones in littered lots and neglected parks and gardens in large cities, but not so much in suburbs. It remains in hiding all day long and forages in late afternoon and evening for slugs, snails, and earthworms, all of which comprise 60 percent of its diet. There are between nine and twenty live-born young in a litter, each just less than ten centimeters long.

The red-bellied snake, just under thirty centimeters in length, varies in colour from gray to dark or light brown, chestnut, or sometimes black. A light stripe, bordered on each side by two dusky lines, and a dark head with the impression of a bright red or pink necklace complete the picture. Unfortunately for the red-bellied snake, some panic-stricken people mistake it for a copperhead. Its habits are similar to the brown snake, except its litter size ranges from one to thirteen, the average being around seven.

Really, your chances of stumbling across a poisonous snake in urban or heavily populated suburban areas in North America are exceedingly small. Various versions of the rattlesnake are found in Ontario, Saskatchewan, Alberta, British Columbia, and all but three states (Hawaii, Alaska, and Maine). Copperheads, water moccasins and coral snakes dwell mainly in the southeastern states, but the coral also resides in southern Arizona. If you should encounter a snake you think is poisonous, you can assure yourself of its status by determining whether the head is wider than the neck (the slender coral snake is an exception). If it is, avoid the snake in question. A deep pit about midway between the eye and the nostril, and a vertically shaped pupil in the eye are also features of poisonous snakes. Non-poisonous snakes have a round pupil. If you've found a dead snake, flip it over. On the underside of the tail, non-poisonous snakes have two rows of scales, while poisonous snakes only have one. The coral snake is ringed with red, yellow and black, but before you start crushing or shooting every snake coloured this way, keep in mind those beneficial mimics of the coral snakes; their red and yellow rings are separated by black ones. You might remember it this way: red on yellow, kill a fellow; red on black, friend of Jack. The best advice, though, is simply to leave them be.

The choice places to find snakes around your home are in and under stacked firewood, old lumber and junk piles, flower beds with heavy mulch, shrubbery growing right against foundations, gardens, unmowed lawns, and abandoned lots and fields, pond and stream banks cluttered with discarded items, and basements and attics crammed with paraphenalia or with rodent or bat problems. Essentially, a cool, dark, damp area will be attractive to snakes.

To keep them out, all openings of 6.4 millimeters or larger must be sealed with either mortar, fine-mesh hardware cloth, or sheet metal, depending on the structure. The corners of doors and windows, spaces around water pipes and electrical service entrances are prime entry points. If you do live in a region frequented by venomous snakes, a snake-proof fence can be constructed either around your yard (it's not cheap, though) or around a play space for children too young to identify poisonous snakes. Contrary to what you might have heard, mothballs are ineffective deterrents.

If you've got a snake problem but you're the kind of person who simply doesn't want to meet up with a snake of any kind, the best solution is to make the habitat unsuitable for them. All sources of rodent food must be kept in secure containers. Similarly, don't leave any pet food lying around. Any possible cover, such as bushes, shrubs, rocks, boards and debris, should be removed.

If you've got a snake problem and you're not particularly frightened by them, you can remove them yourself by placing piles of damp burlap bags near a suspected hangout. After covering the pile with a dry bag, leave them out for a couple of weeks before scooping up the whole pile during midday when the snakes are likely to be inside. You can release them in a nearby park or ravine, but away from other people's homes. Honestly, though, snakes want to see you even less than you want to see them.

Salamanders

Another equally innocuous critter, the red-backed salamander, appears to show a high degree of urban tolerance by requiring less complicated environmental conditions. Although it does need the kind of moisture found in deciduous woods, this salamander lays its eggs in rotting logs rather than in ponds. The young complete their gilled larval stage within the egg and hatch as miniatures of the adults.

Red-backed salamanders are highly intolerant of dryness and excessive heat. Less than 102 millimeters long and, like all salamanders, lacking lungs, it depends on its moist skin and the roof of its mouth for respiration. The stripe on the back may be yellow, orange or gray, but the telltale sign for this species is a belly finely mottled with black and white. In the dryness of mid-summer, red-backed salamanders retreat below ground. During periods of soaking rain in the spring or fall, they may be found under stones and logs or even wandering about in the open, feeding upon a wide variety of insects and invertebrates.

Turtles

Like the snakes, the slow-moving and somewhat defenseless box turtle would also rather avoid you. Most likely to be encountered in suburbia in the United States, the box turtles' biggest problems are avoiding being picked up for pet stock and being squashed on a roadway. Box turtles have really got to be one of the most harmless of all city critters. With a sharp-edged, horny beak that substitutes for teeth, they eat vegetation including mushrooms, berries and leaves, as well as beetles, snails, slugs, crayfish, and caterpillars. Small amphibians and reptiles are also eaten (when they can be caught!). These turtles are not averse to dining on dead animals, either. Interestingly, they're immune to poisonous mushrooms, but any animal feeding on a box turtle that has just consumed such mushrooms will become ill. Like most turtles, they dig holes in soft sand to lay their eggs. These are left unguarded, and once hatched, the young turtles are entirely on their own. Although not well documented, the life span of these turtles is apparently equal to that of humans.

Toads

Toads, in general, seem to be able to tough it out in our cities. They can use almost any body of water to breed in. Since most of their predators and competitors have been eliminated by us, and in spite of large numbers being taken as pets during the toadlet state, some toad species are actually increasing in number.

Toads, with the aid of specially developed hind feet, are able to shuffle themselves down into loose earth, either covering themselves completely or just leaving the top of the head exposed. These voracious feeders eat mainly invertebrates, but will take larger prey as they themselves grow in size. One adult tried to eat a baby red-winged blackbird that had fallen from its nest. Any prey must move first to be spotted. After stalking it methodically, the toad flashes out its tongue, which has a sticky tip, and smoothly flips tongue and prey back into the mouth. Some protruding parts of larger prey might be crammed in with the toad's forelegs. Toads don't waste much, and even eat their own skin after it's been shed.

About those warts: rest assured that toads cannot give you warts! Their warts, along with the paratoid glands, produce a sticky white poison that is highly toxic to some animals. It might render human hands and fingers temporarily numb, but it is essentially harmless to us. Most snakes aren't bothered by it, but dogs picking up toads in their mouths have quickly regretted it.

Toads are shy and solitary and usually just hide out under a step or flat stone, or at the base of a shrub all season long. They're most vocal on warm, humid nights, but do sometimes call out in the daytime. During the breeding season toads congregate in temporary ponds or along the edges of lakes, rivers or streams, where they lay up to eight thousand eggs in two long strips, one from each oviduct.

HONEY··· THE TOADS ARE HAVING A BARBEQUE AGAIN!!

The male deposits his sperm on them to complete fertilization. The tadpoles transform into tiny toadlets between late June and early August. Rapid growth—sometimes they double and triple their size—ensues, and even continues during hibernation below ground (depending on the climate). The mortality rate of the young is quite high; each year only a third of all adult males survive. Toads have been known to reach at least eight years of age in the wild, though. Because of their diet and unobtrusive nature, toads are a fine animal to have around the yard.

Frogs

Although the bullfrog can be heard bellowing in weedy areas along lakes and ponds within city limits, there are two better examples of city-dwelling frogs, and they both originated in Cuba. Limited thus far to southeastern Florida and the Keys, the Cuban or giant tree frog is found in palm and banana trees, shrubbery, and near buildings and cisterns.

The largest of all tree frogs in North America, the females are 12.7 centimeters long and the males 8.9 centimeters. Their rough, moist skin varies in colour from light beige to deep brown or olive. Outstanding features include great glowing eyes and large adhesive disks on their toes.

It's this last characteristic that tends to get them in trouble. Being excellent climbers and jumpers, Cuban tree frogs have caused power failures by scaling hydro poles and straddling two wires on the small transformers. Apparently they only climb up them when the temperatures drops to between 13° and 23° C. The problem can be resolved by installing squirrel guards on the poles and using insulated transformer covers.

Homeowners are apt to find these frogs sitting under their eaves, out of the hot sun. They also lay their eggs in water cisterns and flooded basements. Their insatiable appetite for invertebrates makes them a great backyard companion.

In North America the greenhouse frog takes well to human habitats, especially gardens and greenhouses. This tiny creature lays about twenty eggs under debris, decaying litter, or frequently in and under flowerpots. Unlike most other species, the greenhouse frog sits near its egg cluster. After several days, you can easily see two big peepers looking through the transparent egg membrane. The newly hatched young are not much bigger than the head of a pin.

Well, that's a brief look at some of the more successful reptiles and amphibians of the city. Snakes are faced with a huge public relations problem, while some people find frogs and toads a little noisy at times. Cats and dogs probably kill a good many of the herptiles, and window wells become deadly traps for still others. Surely though our cities and suburbs can provide a little room for these creatures. Besides offering excellent natural pest control, they carry few diseases and are capable of enriching the lives of city dwellers.

Bibliography

Baker, R.H. *Michigan Mammals.* Michigan State University Press, East Lansing, MI, 1983.

Banfield, A.W.F. *The Mammals of Canada.* University of Toronto Press, Toronto, Ont., 1974.

Chapman, J.A. and G.A. Feldhamer (eds.). *Wild Mammals of North America: Biology, Management, and Economics.* Johns Hopkins University Press, Baltimore, MD, 1982.

Cook, F.R. *Introduction to Canadian Amphibians and Reptiles.* National Museums of Canada, Ottawa, 1984.

Degraaf, R.M. and G.M. Witman. *Trees, Shrubs, and Vines for Attracting Birds: A Manual for the Northeast.* University of Massachusetts Press, Amherst, MA, 1979.

Dennis, J.V. *A Complete Guide to Birdfeeding.* Alfred A. Knopf, New York, NY, 1978.

Godin, A.J. *Wild Mammals of New England.* Johns Hopkins University Press, Baltimore, MD, 1977.

Harrison, G.H. *The Backyard Bird Watcher.* Simon and Schuster, New York, NY, 1979.

Lowery, G.H., Jr. *The Mammals of Louisiana and Its Adjacent Waters.* Louisiana State Press, Baton Rouge, LA, 1974.

McKinley, M. *How to Attract Birds.* Ortho Books, Chevron Chemical Co., San Francisco, CA, 1983.

Mumford, R.E. and J.O. Whitaker Jr. *Mammals of Indiana.* Indiana University Press, Bloomington, IN, 1982.

Noyes, J.H. and D.R. Progulske (eds.) *Wildlife in an Urbanizing Environment.* Coop. Extens. Services, Amherst, MA, 1974.

Schwartz, C.W. and E.R. Schwartz. *The Wild Mammals of Missouri.* University of Missouri Press, Columbia, MO, 1981.

Timm, R.M. (ed.) *Prevention and Control of Wildlife Damage.* Institute of Agric. and National Resources, Lincoln, NB, 1983.

(Photo courtesy of the Gazette)

David M. Bird

David was born in Toronto, Ontario, in 1949, and it was there that he developed his strong interest in wildlife. He is particularly fascinated by birds of prey.

Dr. Bird earned his B.Sc. in Zoology from the University of Guelph in 1973, and then transferred to McGill to obtain his M.Sc. in 1976 and his doctorate in wildlife biology in 1978. He has published over fifty papers in scientific journals and serves on dozens of committees dedicated to wildlife biology and conservation at local, national, and international levels.

His keen interest in promoting public awareness of wildlife is exemplified by numerous media appearances, countless public-speaking engagements, and a weekly bird column, "Bird's Eye View," in the Montreal *Gazette*. There is no truth to the rumour that Dr. Bird's name is connected to his chosen career.

(Photo by Joanne Wiggins)

Sandra Letendre

Sandra was born in Quebec City and has freelanced in art since graduating with a B.F.A. from Concordia University, Montreal, in 1980. Work as a naturalist, and a passion for outdoor sports, has allowed her plenty of opportunity to observe the animals that appear in her illustrations.

Growing up, she and her family shared their home with a variety of pet raccoons, snakes, snapping turtles, fish, mice, dogs, and cats. Currently living in Montreal, with no pets of her own, she has, however, achieved remarkable success in training her dustballs to hide under the furniture when company arrives.